DRINK *like a* LOCAL
PARIS

*A Field Guide to
Paris' Best Bars*

Drink Like a Local: Paris
A Field Guide to Paris' Best Bars

13-Digit ISBN: 978-1-64643-457-2
10-Digit ISBN: 1-64643-457-9

This book may be ordered by mail from the publisher. Please include $5.99 for postage and handling. Please support your local bookseller first!

Books published by Cider Mill Press Book Publishers are available at special discounts for bulk purchases in the United States by corporations, institutions, and other organizations. For more information, please contact the publisher.

Cider Mill Press Book Publishers
"Where good books are ready for press"
501 Nelson Place
Nashville, Tennessee 37214

cidermillpress.com

Typography: Ballinger, Condor, Pacifico, Poppins, Stolzl

Printed in Malaysia

23 24 25 26 27 OFF 5 4 3 2 1
First Edition

DRINK *like a* LOCAL
PARIS

A Field Guide to
Paris' Best Bars

FOREST COLLINS

CIDER MILL PRESS

BOOK
PUBLISHERS

CONTENTS

The real secret to drinking like a local in Paris is knowing that it's mostly a state of mind. Café culture is rife here. Aperitifs are a regular practice. A glass of wine is a way of life rather than a luxury. Parisians socialize, start meals, and finish their day with a drink—in moderation, of course. When they are out for a drink, it's usually someplace that is close, good enough, not too expensive, and feels familiar and comfortable. For your average Parisian, that could be just about any neighborhood café.

Drinking in this local way is actually very easy for visitors. Simply find a place nearby that meets those criteria and go a few times. Get to know the staff. On one of my earliest visits to Paris, my friends and I repeatedly stopped into the café bar on the ground floor of our cheap and cheerful hotel. The place was nothing special, with a generic decor and a dingy appearance. But getting to know the bartender changed everything. He would greet us as we came and went, give us advice about the neighborhood, and happily hand us the coin-like tokens to unlock the Turkish toilet. The feeling that we had a "friend" in France made the bar that much better—in some ways better than a fancy destination bar.

A few years later, I stopped into a hole in the wall Marais bar regularly enough during my trip that I ended up taking part in late-night after-hour hangs. I met a friend at that same bar about ten years later, at which point it had become successful enough to buy the neighboring restaurant space and open a big terrace in front. But the bartender was still there and, a decade later, came out to the terrace, did a surprised double take when he saw me, and then greeted me—by name!

On March 16, 2005, just after moving to Paris, I stepped into the first bar I would drink in *as* a local rather than *like* a local. I chose Lush with the strategy outlined above: it was near my apartment, looked good enough, and not too expensive. That night I got to talking with one of the owners, who encouraged me to come back the next day and meet their bar manager, who he was sure I would become fast friends with. Today, she's still my closest friend in Paris and her middle child is my goddaughter. I've been to marriages, milestone birthdays, special celebrations, and funerals of friends I made as a regular in this off-the-beaten-path pub. A large core of my social group today is either from my time in that bar or thanks to friends I made there.

The bar has changed, and different staff work there since I lived close enough to drop by daily. Now new "regulars" are forging lifelong friendships there and learning that so much of what makes a real Parisian drinking experience special and authentic is this perfect storm of place, people, and time—and your state of mind.

This doesn't mean there aren't local destination bars in Paris worth crossing town
for. There most definitely are and that's why
I wrote this book. I'm genuinely excited to
share all of these unique places and the
stories that tie them to this city and its
culture. I'm happy to give visitors a glimpse
into the great diversity of venues and the
locals who frequent them. Paris is a melting
pot of born and bred French, immigrants,
and expats from all over, which is reflected
in the drinks scene.

So, I hope you enjoy the places suggested
on these pages. And, if you really want to
drink like a local, I also hope you find your
own Lush somewhere on the side streets of
the city.

1st & 2nd Arrondissements
Saint-Honoré / Louvre / Rivoli

In the very heart of the city, the first and second arrondissements cover some high-priced historical real estate. Here you'll find luxury hotel bars and upscale cocktail lounges that fit right in. But you can also find dusty, divey joints if you know where to look.

17th

16th

7t

15th

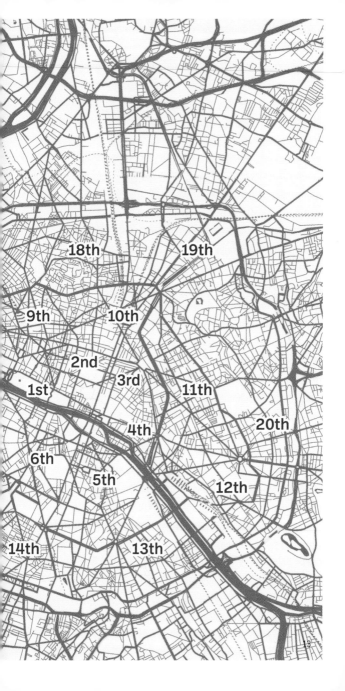

REHAB

7 Rue de l'Échelle, 75001 Paris

You don't just stumble into this sexy speakeasy. You actively seek it out. Head to the historic Hotel Normandy and ask the night guard to take you to Rehab. You'll be led through the building and down a small iron spiral staircase into an otherworldly subterranean hideaway.

Before you even order a drink, the ambience alone will induce a state of relaxation. Low lighting, chandeliers, silk curtains, paper lanterns, and distressed walls lend a dreamlike drama to the decor. An antique imported opium bed invites clients to fully indulge in the fantasy of escaping the everyday.

Cocktails come in vessels like Chinese vases or smoking teapots, which only adds to the theatrical spell. Rehab doesn't serve food so it's an ideal place in which to impress a date for pre- or post-dinner drinks or have a confidential catch up with your BFF. Prices are higher than the average bar but well worth the cost for the guaranteed escape from the urban bustle and standing-room-only spots. While frequented largely by a young professional crowd, Rehab is a welcoming and comfortable venue for cocktail lovers of all ages.

The hush-hush address plus a few fringe ingredients add to the illusion of the illicit. A very small portion of the bar's cocktail menu uses cannabidiol in drinks via oils, infusions, or smoke. This chemical compound is more commonly known as CBD, found in marijuana. Unlike THC, which is mainly what causes the drug's psychological effects, CBD is supposed to help you relax without the pesky paranoia and high. However, this ingredient is highlighted in only a few cocktails and the bar's main focus is on a quality mixology program.

FLY ME TO THE MOON

3½ oz. vodka

5 oz. Amaretto

1¾ oz. fresh lemon juice

3½ oz. verjus

5 oz. brewed coffee

3½ oz. simple syrup

¼ cup Biscoff Spread

6 oz. whole milk

1. Combine all of the ingredients in a container with a lid, mix well, and refrigerate overnight.
2. The following day, strain the mixture into a bottle, using a coffee filter over a fine mesh sieve.
3. Keep refrigerated to serve over ice when the spirit strikes. An optional garnish is a powdered dark chocolate rim.

EXPERIMENTAL COCKTAIL CLUB

37 Rue Saint-Sauveur, 75002 Paris

You simply can't talk about craft cocktails in Paris without referencing the forerunner of the local modern mixology movement: Experimental Cocktail Club (ECC). The founders of this industrially chic lounge sought inspiration from New York aughts hotspots like Pegu Club and Milk & Honey and brought a new kind of drinking culture to Paris in 2007, single-handedly leveraging the cocktail renaissance in the French capital.

While Prohibition-inspired drinks and discrete doorways may be old hat by now, this small venue with a giant reputation still manages to pull in a beautiful night-crawling crowd. Not only was this bar the catalyst for craft cocktails in France, but it's also the first venue in what is now an Experimental global hospitality empire, comprising restaurants, bars, and hotels in Venice, New York, London, Majorca, and more. These entrepreneurs know how to discover something worthwhile, add their own French touch, and take it to the next level.

Short lines at the door and the occasional bouncer mean the bar is not as hidden as it once was. Inside, it's minimalistically rustic and cool with heavy velvet drapes, comfy sofas, dim lights, exposed brick, and wooden beams.

The cocktail menu changes seasonally, featuring new house creations and the occasional ECC classic like the Old Cuban. This is also the kind of bar where you can feel completely comfortable ordering a classic. The menu also features the foodie favorite Billecart-Salmon Champagne. All the usual cocktail accoutrements and touches that we've come to expect are present and accounted for: stylish glassware, cut glass flacons, quality spirits, bitters, and fresh garnishes and juices. No food is served, other than the dishes of salty almonds that come with the drinks.

ECC is on the pedestrian-only Rue Saint-Sauveur, which is bursting with bars and small food shops making it easy to spend a full evening here for a fun bar crawl punctuated by snack stops in hip little restaurants for fish and chips, couscous, or trendy gluten-free options.

EXPERIENCE 1

1 lemongrass stalk

2 basil leaves

1⅔ oz. vodka

⅔ oz. elderflower liqueur

⅔ oz. fresh lemon juice

2½ teaspoons simple syrup

1. Chop one-third of the lemongrass stalk and reserve the remaining part of the stalk for garnish.

2. Combine all of the ingredients in a cocktail shaker with ice, shake well for 15 to 20 seconds, and strain into a chilled cocktail glass.

3. Garnish with the remainder of the lemongrass stalk.

HARRY'S NEW YORK BAR

5 Rue Daunou, 75002 Paris

With a history tightly entwined with the city's Anglophone drinking population, Harry's Bar pulls in a fair number of tourists. Back in the day, they even advertised in the international press that visitors should tell their taxi driver to take them straight to "Sank Roo Doe Noo" (the phonetic pronunciation of their address). But today plenty of locals still belly up to this bar. The French head here for a taste of Americana, and American expats crowd in for the annual US elections straw poll, which has rarely been off. In-the-know locals slip through the crowded main floor to the refined, lesser-known downstairs piano bar for an elegant evening cocktail.

Its original name, "New York Bar," gives a nod to the provenance of its heavy dark wood bar, which was dismantled in 1911 and shipped to Paris from its former NYC location. It became Harry's New York Bar when it was taken over by its famous head barman, Harry MacElhone. Harry's has seen plenty of well-known expats at its counter: Hemingway, Fitzgerald, and Gershwin, to name a few. It also spawned the creation of its own historically renowned society of serious drinkers, the IBF (International Bar Flies.)

Cocktail enthusiasts come to soak up the history and order something featured in its revered recipe book from the 1920s, *Harry's ABC of Mixing Cocktails*, such as a White Lady, Scofflaw, or Side Car. And, while its true creator is often disputed, the Bloody Mary will forever be linked with this bar, which claims to have invented it.

Expect old school bartenders in crisp white shirts, black ties, and serious demeanors to serve up one of 400 cocktails or 350 whiskies on offer. The comfy red booths are packed with jolly drinkers from all walks and American college pennants cover the walls—and have even inspired a recent spinoff line of preppy Harry's sweats and jackets.

Still owned by the MacElhone family, Harry's is history, legend, and American and French patrons all shaken together to make for one very famous cocktail.

SCOFFLAW

This cocktail was invented at Harry's in response to the coining of the term "scofflaw" during Prohibition in the United States to describe someone who drinks.

1½ oz. rye whiskey

1 oz. dry vermouth

¾ oz. fresh lime juice

½ oz. grenadine

1 dash orange bitters

1. Combine all of the ingredients in a cocktail shaker with ice, shake well for 10 to 15 seconds, and strain into a chilled cocktail glass.

DANICO

6 Rue Vivienne, 75002 Paris

Danico is one of the city's more stylish and successful bars, thanks in large part to its talented owner, Nico de Soto. This Parisian-born industry powerhouse is a world traveler—104 countries at last count—pop-up organizer, consultant, and owner of the NYC cocktail bar Mace. His globetrotting and global projects inspire, inform, and infuse his home turf project.

Danico is compact, chic, and simply oozes stylish adult sensibility. This is where the real grown-ups go for a serious drink. The space was originally the Jean Paul Gaultier flagship shop, and a nod to JPG is seen in the snappy nautical shirts worn by the sharp-dressed staff.

Boldly patterned wallpaper, rich colors, velvet uphol-stery, and a tiny mezzanine set the scene. Large side windows let in enough light to properly illuminate the gold shakers and clinking glasses in all the right ways.

In the daytime, enter through the iconic Gallerie Vivienne covered arcade that dates from 1823. In the evening, head through the big, bustling trattoria, Darocco. This Italian eatery is connected to the bar and funnels in paired-up locals looking for a pre- or post-dinner drink. The stools at the bar are usually filled with solo sippers or cocktail enthusiasts exploring the intriguing menu.

De Soto brings a lot of flavor from his voyages to the cocktails. He pretty much single-handedly introduced the mixology world to the use of pandan, a tropical plant found in south and southeast Asia with a unique flavor profile of grassy sweetness. And it's not just inspired ingredients that set Danico apart but also skilled techniques and the use of equipment like sous vide to intensify flavor.

Not only has de Soto worked at some of the best bars in the world, he has also gained his own acclaim, being named most influential industry personality by both Cocktails Spirits and *Drinks International*. He's even

launched his own line of cocktail tools. The de Soto double teardrop stirrer showcases his skills in excelling simultaneously at form and function. And that pretty much sums up Danico as well.

TIPSY LUWAK

This cocktail was created by Danico's owner, Nico de Soto, who pretty much single-handedly kicked off the craze for pandan as a cocktail ingredient.

2⅔ oz. Japanese whisky (preferably Nikka From the Barrel)

1 avocado

⅔ oz. coconut milk

1 teaspoon coconut water

1 teaspoon Indonesian coffee

2 oz. Pandan Syrup

1. Combine all of the ingredients in a blender and blend until combined.
2. Pour 4 oz. into a glass filled with crushed ice and garnish with a pandan leaf.

Pandan Syrup (this large-batch recipe can be halved or quartered for smaller portions): Gently heat 5¼ cups palm sugar with 2 cups plus 1 tablespoon water, stirring until dissolved. Add 8 pandan leaves and ⅔ teaspoon salt. Continue heating the mixture for 30 minutes, using a kitchen thermometer to maintain a temperature of 140°F. Cool, strain, and store.

LE RUBIS

10 Rue du Marché Saint-Honoré, 75001 Paris

Almost everyone visiting Paris wants to uncover the city's authentic side. Most of the places where they find "local color" are a bit polished up and already discovered by plenty of other tourists. But, Le Rubis gives a real glimpse into French life, and I almost hesitate to share it to ensure it always stays the same.

At first glance, you may not appreciate what makes this restaurant with a dusty red awning so special. Worn wine barrels on either side of the door serve as outdoor tables during peak hours. The tabletops and flooring haven't had a refresh in years. But, look a little closer and those hexagonal floor tiles recall the Provençal *tomette* tiles made from terracotta and are *très* French. The bar top? Classic zinc. Old-school plastic signage serves more as inspiration than actual information since they feature lists of wine regions and bottles no longer on offer with no prices.

No need for a menu, though, as you just ask the brusque but friendly enough barman what's open. Whatever you order will run around a fiver and go very well with one of their superb charcuterie boards of *saucisson sec*, chunky terrine, and creamy butter.

Go midafternoon between meal services when diehards stand at the bar (no stools), chatting and joking. It's a mostly male clientele that seems to be all old friends. Or to have just become firm friends after a glass or two. Later, Le Rubis picks up its pace with regulars who stop in for a quick pick-me-up or crowd the sidewalk for aperitif hour, which sometimes morphs into a makeshift dinner.

Le Rubis also does a respectable service for lunch or dinner with dishes like *œufs en meurette*, boudin, or steak frites. And a real unexpected treat is the Japanese toilet, which is not what you'd hope to find in such a no-frills spot.

In short, you go here to practice your French and hang with unpretentious locals. It can be a little intimidating for the uninitiated, but it's well worth the effort to step up to this bar.

LE BAISER SALÉ

58 Rue des Lombards, 75001 Paris

The bar of Le Baiser Salé, a live music venue that's less polished than the more upscale jazz bars in the area, like Duc des Lombards, attracts a frenetic crowd to its terrace for the 3 to 9 p.m. cheap and cheerful happy hour. They feature many talented musicians who play evening sets of Afro, Antilles, and fusionstyles of jazz in the upstairs club. While the musical program has a strong reputation, the service, drinks, and crowd can be more of a mixed bag. But that's all part of its appeal—as long as you're prepared for it.

Beyond the busy terrace, a more motley group of patrons settles around the heavy wood horseshoe bar in the dark downstairs area for beers, ti' punches, or *rhum arrangé*. Neon signs give off a red glow and concert posters and portraits of musicians hang on the wooden walls. Here you'll find jazz aficionados waiting for the later sets alongside more questionable characters ordering something stiff, or local and international youngsters sampling small beers and beverages that may be bright blue and sweet.

This is the kind of place you want to order something easy like a lager or a simple rhum agricole served neat. Slowly sip your drink and soak in the atmosphere. The bar stays open until 6 a.m., so service can be super or surly, depending on the time and temperament of whomever is behind the bar.

This place isn't fancy but it's definitely got a distinct personality—one that, much like the meaning of its name ("Salty Kiss" in English), can be both sweet and surprisingly strange. It's a good reminder that Paris locals like locales of all different stripes. And, if you want to enjoy a bit of the live jazz, they sell a concert pass plus champagne on their site, as well as branded black T-shirts and water bottles should you want to bring a souvenir of this side of Paris back home.

2nd Arrondissement
3-Stop Barhop

NIGHT FLIGHT
18 Rue Bachaumont, 75002 Paris

JEFREY'S
14 Rue Saint-Sauveur, 75002 Paris

GOLDEN PROMISE
11 Rue Tiquetonne, 75002 Paris

For a fun little barhop in the area, stop into Night Flight, Jefrey's, and Golden Promise, which are all within easy walking distance of one another and offer three different ways to drink like a local—in a sophisticated hotel bar, a cocktail lounge, and a venue dedicated entirely to whisky.

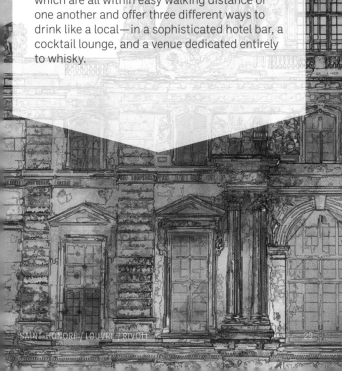

3rd & 4th Arrondissements
Marais / Haute Marais

Marais has plenty of historical charm but it's also a hotbed for fashionably hip bars, boutiques, and eateries, so there are plenty of trendy spots for a tipple.

17th

16th

7t

15th

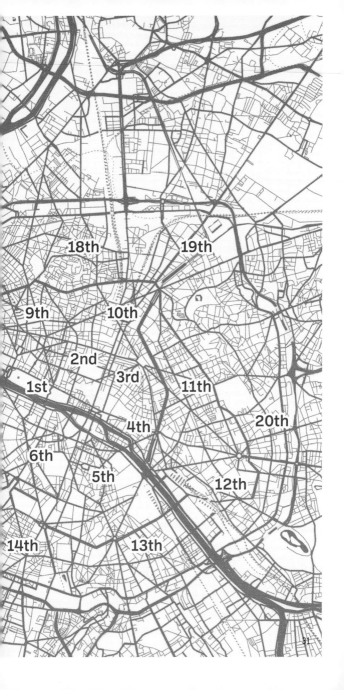

18th

19th

9th

10th

2nd

1st

3rd

11th

4th

20th

6th

5th

12th

14th

13th

LITTLE RED DOOR

60 Rue Charlot, 75003 Paris

Awhimsically small door marks the otherwise unassuming entrance to one of the city's famous bars, Little Red Door. Though its decorative door may be small, its reputation is anything but as this bar holds its own on the global cocktail scene.

LRD is well-known for a series of conceptual bar menus that focus on such lofty concepts as architecture or art. Having worked through several of these inspired cocktail collections successfully, the team has settled into a real sweet spot with their current menu direction, farm to glass. They now showcase French farmers and passionate local producers, shining a spotlight on their quality ingredients. And what better country in which to celebrate terroir than France?

This locavore tendency has spurred rather than stifled creativity and they keep, in their own words, "playfully pushing boundaries" when it comes to drinks. The recognition and accolades they've received indicate they are doing so successfully.

So successfully, in fact, that there is often a long line of thirsty customers waiting to drink in some of that creativity. Meaning: reservations are recommended when possible. Once you make it past the friendly doorman, you'll find yourself in an intimate and discrete space decorated with custom and handpicked pieces.

Jewel-tone upholstery pops against the exposed brick and stone walls. One of my favorite things about this bar are the ultra-comfy plush bar stools—as if the drinks alone weren't enough to keep you sitting there. The glassware is unique, with much of it created custom for each new menu.

LRD's strongest asset is the team's willingness to adapt, evolve, and strive for more. They keep things fresh by regularly inviting guest bartenders and stay inspired by traveling to explore other bars and cultures. In addition to going local, they keep a focus on ecologically sound practices and are always looking for ways to get products from nearby farms to the bar in greener ways.

Little Red Door has gradually and thoughtfully evolved since its conception, taking an already solid concept and tweaking it into something even better.

FARMHOUSE SOUR

Adding a cider from Brittany to this drink is in line with how Little Red Door celebrates French ingredients and local producers.

½ egg white or ½ tbsp. aquafaba

1⅓ oz. malt whisky

1 oz. Breton cider

⅓ oz. simple syrup

¼ oz. verjus

1. Add the egg white or aquafaba to a cocktail shaker and dry shake for 10 seconds.

2. Add the remaining ingredients to the shaker, fill halfway with ice, shake well for 10 to 15 seconds, and strain into a chilled cocktail glass.

3. Optional garnish: grated cured egg yolk.

CANDELARIA

52 Rue de Saintonge, 75003 Paris

This agave focused bar was one of the forerunners of the craft cocktail renaissance in Paris. Co-owners Carina Soto Velasquez and Joshua Fontaine had already made noteworthy names for themselves working at the ECC group bars (see page 16) before opening this speakeasy hidden behind a tiny taqueria.

The kitchen up front serves tasty tacos made from scratch. Go early to snag one of the few stools at the counter of this minuscule, bustling taqueria. It's not easy to find good Mexican in Paris, so you're likely to be bumping elbows with homesick North American expats looking for familiar flavors. Once finished, those with a penchant for a party will confidently head for the unmarked door at the back of the room to slip into the dim, candlelit Candelaria.

Candelaria has received many awards and much press coverage for their cocktail program, both domestically and internationally. This means you are likely to find cocktail-minded locals as well as visiting industry folks. The place packs out quickly—thus the doorman during peak hours. Going right at opening increases chances for a quiet cocktail hour or a deeper exploration of the long list of agave spirits with guidance from the staff.

And the agave is how this bar really sets itself apart. A mezcal menu lists out dozens of options categorized by flavor profile and finishes. They also feature Mexican

spirits and drinks that you won't find elsewhere in Paris, like raicilla, pulque, and sotol.

There is more than Mexican spirits though,—this is the bar that birthed the spicy modern classic Guèpe Verte. Rather than resting on these laurels, they continue to evolve and express new things with their creations.

GUÊPE VERTE

In Candelaria's early days they created the refreshingly spicy Guêpe Verte, which quickly became a contemporary classic.

1¾ oz. Chile-Infused Tequila

1 tablespoon agave syrup (1:1)

1 tablespoon fresh lime juice

5 cilantro leaves

1 cucumber slice

1. Combine all of the ingredients in a cocktail shaker with ice, shake well for 10 to 15 seconds, and strain into a rocks glass over ice.

2. Garnish with a cucumber ribbon.

Chile-Infused Tequila: Halve 2 or 3 chiles, add them to a bottle of blanco tequila, and let stand for 24 hours. Strain and store.

CAMBRIDGE PUBLIC HOUSE

8 Rue de Poitou, 75003 Paris

Cambridge Public House is a happy confluence of two cultures: a modern-day British pub with French sensibilities. While Paris has no shortage of standard corner cafés where the masses regularly meet, sometimes locals want a change of pace. The pub, much like the French café, is the culture's everyday drinking and meeting place, so the team has imported the British version of the "third place" and given it the French touch.

These publicans lighten up the traditional dark green and wood decor with plants, ceiling fans, and tall window walls that are open on warm days to welcome in the fresh air and sunlight. Traditional paintings of boats and hunting dogs hang on the walls, and playful hound sculptures hold up rounds of wood to serve as side tables.

Pull up a stool at the bar or grab a table with a group of friends to work through the range of perfectly poured pints and the gastropub dishes, like meat pies or sausage rolls made with seasonal local ingredients.

But it's not just pub grub and pints. Cambridge has a solid cocktail program that also relies on seasonal ingredients, and the menu regularly rotates drinks based on what's fresh and available. The Cambridge also engages in a cocktail practice that you see in very few

Paris bars: the Tiny Bev. This is a menu of mini cocktails at lower prices, making it easy to sample a few and still walk home in a straight line. It's also an option that appeals to a certain demographic of French drinkers who are still coming around to the strength of a stiff classic cocktail.

Another reason for the success of this communal space is the early opening hours. Like pubs and cafés, there's no need to wait for typically later opening hours of many of the city's serious cocktail bars.

Since its conception, the team has worked to make Cambridge Public House a community hub. And they are now reinforcing this idea of community at a global level as well, through different initiatives like their current mission to help countries around the world implement six of the seventeen United Nations Sustainable Development Goals.

DELICATE NIRVANA

Cambridge Public House is one of the few bars in Paris serving mini-cocktails. This twist on a Tuxedo from their Tiny Bev menu is perfect for dry martini lovers. This recipe is for a larger batch that can be bottled and stored in the fridge for up to three weeks and then served in tiny or regular-sized portions at your leisure.

3⅓ oz. London dry gin

3⅓ oz. saké

3⅓ oz. dry white vermouth

4 teaspoons umeshu

12 dashes ponzu sauce

1. Either stir all of the ingredients in a mixing glass over ice to dilute or add 4 ounces water to the ingredients and then pour into a bottle and refrigerate.

SERPENT À PLUME

24 Pl. des Vosges, 75003 Paris

Just off Paris' oldest square, Place des Vosges, the relatively unassuming Serpent à Plume restaurant hides a highly curated basement bar with Wes Anderson vibes and its own manifesto. Here's where you might find the bourgeois French bohemian wearing expensive silk pajamas as evening wear.

The manifesto proclaims that "unconventional programming and aesthetic universe is the ultimate manifestation of how we create community." Sure, that feels vaguely art-speak, but the entire ethos here is that fashion, not real life, reigns.

This "experience" is the creation of Alex Rash, a twenty-first century dandy who knows how to pair a trendy blue suit with a knit stocking cap and pull it off with style. He made his way to France from Minneapolis, Minnesota, eventually finding his way into the fashion world. The sartorial creator of this surreal little world made a space where "cats, thieves, and illicit lovers lose themselves to the music and food as they leave reality behind." Whatever that means.

But as nonconformist as that sounds, it's still a space where you'll find Parisian socialites. The press says a lot about the clientele of this place. While it hasn't made much headway in the international English-speaking press, Rash and his role in Serpent have a large spread in the local online magazine that celebrates the successful social set, "The Socialite Family: A Sample of Smart and Cool Families." *Oui*, this is the kind of concept project where the well-heeled Frenchies will likely relish speaking English with their delicate continental accents.

Serpent à Plume is visually entertaining, with shiny white vinyl sofas juxtaposed against the original vaulted walls, Mesoamerican sculptures against jewel-toned velour stools. It's a cleverly crafted fantasy of adventure, escape, and laissez-faire attitude.

The cocktails are fun and not as expensive as you might expect for such a tony location. Some evenings there are DJs or jazz and between live music and their background soundtrack, things can get a little loud. So, go early if you prefer a quieter peek at this part of Parisian life. Also, I haven't had the occasion to see it but I hear there is a jacuzzi hidden on the premises.

LE 1905

25 Rue Beautreillis, 75004 Paris

While not entirely hidden, the entrance to this bar above a busy Paris neo-bistro is discrete enough to discourage the uncertain, keeping the magical location somewhat of an insider secret.

This accessibly under-the-radar bar is located in an area with some interesting French history. It's on Rue Beautreillis, the street where famed French poet Baudelaire once lived and Cézanne had a studio. Jim Morrison also lived—and died—on this street. The restaurant beneath the bar has been around since 1905, under different owners, but the same name: Vins des Pyrenees. The original sign is still in use today.

1905 is located in what was once the home of the same family for three generations. The large apartment was not entirely gutted, which creates a feeling of intimacy, notwithstanding the rather large space, thanks to separate areas or rooms.

Owner, Florian Cadiou, sought inspiration from his background in both restaurants and acting to make 1905 a magical escape from the everyday. Romantic flea-market sourced seating like heavy dark chesterfield sofas, jewel-toned chaises longues, and a pretty rattan princess chair make it easy to sink into the experience of getting away from it all.

An intimate, lush balcony terrace with twinkling string lights and plenty of leafy plants provides further escape

within the escape. The smoking room, with its burgundy walls covered in old portraits and velour armchairs huddled around a marble-topped fireplace, feels exactly like the kind of place to which one retires after dinner. Worth noting for the nonsmokers: ventilation is good so you don't get a lot of smoky smells wafting into the rest of the space.

Sit at the small bar and order beer, wine, or champagne, the latter being an appropriate choice for a venue that celebrates respite. Don't overlook the cocktails, which both taste and look good. Its location above a trendy restaurant is a real bonus since it means you can snack on small dishes from the downstairs menu.

And, while I haven't been, word is that their occasional themed roaring 1920s soirees are a real treat.

LES BAINS
ROXO

7 Rue du Bourg l'Abbé, 75003 Paris

Much like Studio 54 defined an era in New York City nightlife, Les Bains Douches did so for Paris. Housed in what was previously the city's first spa, opened in 1885, Les Bains Douches was an iconic nocturnal playground for the city's party people of the 1970s, '80s and '90s. Owners left the pool from the original spa in the middle of the club and tipsy, daring disco divas and dudes would take late-night dips in the middle of promiscuous parties. In its heyday, this club counted the likes of Iggy Pop, Mick Jagger, Yves Saint Laurent, and a young Johnny Depp and Kate Moss as regulars. Supermodels and the super elite would groove to the tunes of the then up-and-coming DJ David Guetta in this Philippe Stark designed space. Alas, tastes and times change, and this force of French nightlife closed its doors in 2010.

Luckily for those seeking some nostalgic replay of a gritty-glam bygone era, the location has been over-hauled and revamped into something more of this time, but with a reminder of its edgy past. Now simply known as Les Bains, this space includes a smaller version of the dance club, with a pool and also a hotel, restaurant, and a stand-alone bar, the Roxo. Here you can order creative cocktails or go classic. And while the bartenders pride themselves on their well-made mixed drinks, this is definitely the kind of venue to slip into something indulgent like a bottle of bubbles.

Roxo pulls in both a more mature crowd that would rather linger over upscale cocktails than make it past the late-night scrutiny of doormen downstairs and club-bers starting off with a few sips to pass the time before arriving at a fashionably late hour below. Drinks are a little more expensive than average, which is normal in a venue of this nature, with its storied pedigree and upscale hotel location.

A drink at Roxo is a perfect way to get close to the legendary grit and glamor of the old Les Bains Douches but without having to stay up past your bedtime.

L'EPICIER

24 Rue Notre Dame de Nazareth, 75003 Paris

What appears to be a late-night grocer selling North African goods and sundries like Tunisian harissa and bright boxes of couscous is actually the secret entrance to one of Paris's more popular speakeasies. VGroup, the same team that created the city's other popular and conceptual speakeasy—Lavomatic, which you enter via a washing machine inside a working coin-operated laundromat—is responsible for this *Arabian Nights*–inspired fantasy. Pull the right item off the shelf and it swings open to allow access to their hidey-hole bar.

L'Epicier is dim with moody lighting coming from the many different colors of souk-sourced hanging lanterns. Tables are fashioned from faux stop signs with the word "STOP" written in both English and Arabic. Two rattan chairs dangle from the ceiling, making a sweet little corner for a tête-à-tête.

The cocktails are created with an eye to form and served in interesting vessels or topped with pretty garnishes. Doubling down on the North African inspirations, a popular cocktail is served from a Moroccan teapot in typical fashion, i.e., poured from a good height into a small glass. Ingredients touch on these regional tastes too, with flavors like cardamom, rose water, and orange blossom. It's also just as easy to chill here with a glass of quaffable wine, beer, or a soft drink.

Like its big sister establishment, this bar has received plenty of French press from *TimeOut Paris* to *Elle* magazine, so every twenty-something Parisian who wants to see and be seen in the most Instagrammable spots regularly waits in long lines. This kind of kills the speak-easy illusion, so go as early as possible to experience the intended spirit of this cute little spot.

More Local Favorites

ANDY WAHOO
69 Rue des Gravilliers, 75003 Paris

SHAKE N' SMASH
87 Rue de Turbigo, 75003 Paris

HERBARIUM
243 Rue Saint-Martin, 75003 Paris

LA MEZCALERIA
13 Bd du Temple, 75003 Paris

BISOU
15 Bd du Temple, 75003 Paris

LE MARY CELESTE
1 Rue Commines, 75003 Paris

MARIA LOCA
31 Bd Henri IV, 75004 Paris

SHERRY BUTT
20 Rue Beautreillis, 75004 Paris

5th & 14th Arrondissements
Latin Quarter / Luxembourg / Montparnasse

This covers both the Sorbonne University and a lot of residential real estate, so expect plenty of standard cafés and student haunts, which can almost seem interchangeable. But a handful of bars differentiate themselves here with some very distinct personalities.

17th

16th

7

15th

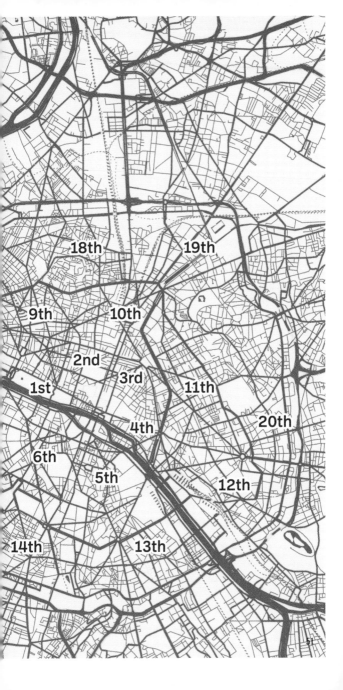

18th

19th

9th

10th

2nd

1st

3rd

11th

4th

20th

6th

5th

12th

14th

13th

SOLERA

283 Rue Saint-Jacques, 75005 Paris

This off-the-beaten path Left Bank cocktail lounge is where you go for showstopper cocktail staging. Founder and bar manager Christopher Gaglione had previously carved out a reputation for his inventive drinks delivery while working behind the bar of the luxury hotel Prince de Galles. At Solera, he combines his high-end service skills and presentation panache in a venue that's just a little more laid-back.

Here you might get the theatrics of a cocktail served in a glass bird under a copper cage, or the playfulness of adorable strawberry-shaped cups and whale tail vessels. Think fun drinks with clever names like the popular Kraken rum-based Poulpe Fiction, served in a glass held in the tentacle of a life-sized, smoke-emitting metal octopus—or *poulpe* in French.

The concept is more than a bar, but what they call a "food-drink" experience, in which elevated snacks can be paired with cocktails. Even with the spectacle of the custom drinkware and unexpected props, the cocktail prices are very reasonable. If you want to just go old school, you can also get a classic martini or Manhattan for around a tenner.

Stepping into Solera is like walking into a designer apartment. Statement wallpaper and an overstuffed velour sofa soften the clean, smooth lines of metal-edged cocktail tables. The whole aesthetic is made especially arresting by the intense peacock color palette of deep blues, greens, and bright gold.

While some tourists in the area wander through, it's remote enough to mean it's often just a destination for locals—where you go for an adult drink with a side of whimsy. Other aspects that make it easier to snag a seat here are the earlier opening hours and an online reservations system. All of this makes for a cool but more comfortable place for drinkers young and old versus some of the packed establishments favored by a young and trendy demographic.

1802

22 Rue Pascal, 75005 Paris

Whether you want to seriously geek out over rum or simply enjoy it in a daiquiri, head to the city's only bar dedicated solely to this spirit.

Located in the Hotel Monte Cristo, 1802 is an elegant bar with some 1,000 types of rum, originally curated in consultation with Alexandre Vigntier, local spirits expert, co-founder of *Rumporter* magazine, and author of the book *101 rhums à découvrir*. The bar hosts master classes on the subject, and the hotel itself has been running an annual Rhum Society event that brings together producers to showcase their spirits in the Monte Cristo's various rooms and suites.

While they have barely any other spirits, they do have interesting rum-adjacent offerings like tafia or cachaça. This is where you go to not just enjoy, but to learn more about rum, if you are so inclined. The knowledgeable staff walks clients through the three different types— rum, ron, and rhum—and helps navigate its many different expressions.

For instance, this is a particularly interesting location for learning more about rhum agricole, which is likely more familiar to locals than those outside of France. This spirit is made from sugarcane juice, rather than molasses, and is under French AOC protection in Martinique. Agricole style rhum is also produced on other French Caribbean islands and is firmly rooted in French culture and history there.

Work through their flights of three or six spirits for a more pedantic approach. Otherwise, order a classic or something from the small menu of rum-forward house cocktails.

While the single-spirit aspect is definitely a draw for rum lovers, 1802 is also a pleasant venue full of eye-catching tiles and leafy plants. A freestanding sleek wood bar offers plenty of counter space for those wanting face time with the bartenders. Otherwise, comfortable chairs and cocktails tables all around the room let sippers contemplate the calm.

The bar name reveals a final French connection, being the birth year of Alexandre Dumas, author of the hotel's namesake novel, *The Count of Monte Cristo*.

LA LUCHA LIBRE

10 Rue de la Montagne Ste Geneviève, 75005 Paris

You either have to be a local or a real wrestling aficionado to know that Paris' La Lucha Libre is the only bar in the country—in Europe, they claim!—with a boxing ring for both organized events and first-come-first-served open matches for customers.

Expect the full technicolor pop culture phenomenon imported from Mexico. Luchodores in brightly colored cartoonish masks step into the ring and partake in their version of wrestling for both sport and entertainment. These battles can go from serious to seriously comic and it's advised to stay a fair distance from the ropes as part of the show sometimes involves taking a sip of beer and then spraying it over the spectators.

In addition to more "professional" wrestlers, La Lucha Libre also keeps two inflatable sumo suits on hand. Eager patrons put these on prior to getting into the ring and bouncing off each, the ropes, and the floor. These costumes have undoubtedly been worn by plenty of wannabe wrestlers, so I suggest spectator support rather than full immersion. Although I've been told it's a fun way to blow off steam should you dare to don the suit.

The wrestling ring is in the basement and really is the main reason to make your way to La Lucha Libre. The upstairs bar is mainly Mexican fiesta appropriation with bright colors, decorative wrestling tchotchkes, and Day of the Dead skulls. The drinks are cheap, with pints of beer often being your best choice. Otherwise, cocktails come with names like Adios Amigo and ingredients like Red Bull. This lively little spot is not far from the Latin Quarter with its university campus and housing, so students often head here for the cheap happy hour and shots. As you might guess in a place like this, service can be fun or spotty, depending on who's behind the bar.

They are only open Wednesday through Saturday and it's certainly a far cry from karaoke for an interactive drinking experience. But, if this sounds like your thing, consider La Lucha Libre your Parisian go-to for both hilarity and hangovers.

ROSEBUD

11 Rue Delambre, 75014 Paris

One of the things that makes living in Paris so special is the history that's part of the city's daily life. So many of the landmarks, boulevards, and buildings hail from another era and afford a glimpse into the capital's past. You can easily slip into a Montmartre café previously frequented by members of the Lost Generation, like Hemingway or Fitzgerald, back in the 1920s. And, sure, this can be an exciting way to celebrate another era, but you're likely to be surrounded by all the other tourists seeking that same peek into bygone times. However, just steps off the main drag of Montmartre Boulevard, it is possible to go back in time in a more under the radar way at the wonderfully retro Rosebud.

The front of the Rosebud is rather unassuming and inside is an elegantly simple classic bar with wooden panels and dim lights. When it opened midcentury it was frequented by Parisian residents with artistic, literary, and philosophical bents like Giacometti, Sartre, and Beauvoir. The name has its own literary ambitions, inspired by Orson Welles' *Citizen Kane*. Not much has changed over the decades in this *Mad Men* meets Montmartre venue, and that's exactly how the locals like it. It's a lovely little gem hidden in plain sight.

Cocktails are a little spendier than average but worth it. They are served by proper old-school staff in crisp whites who can stir and shake creative drinks or classics with gravitas. You can also get a nice selection of wine or a few different beers. As with all good classy

French bars, drinks come with little dishes of salty and crunchy snacks like chips, nuts, or olives.

Rosebud has no website or social media presence. You get the impression that they are happy to only be found by the kind of clientele that will appreciate and maintain their air of cool, quiet authenticity. And that's totally refreshing these days.

Student Hangs in the 5th

LE CROCODILE
6 Rue Royer-Collard, 75005 Paris

LE PANTALON
7 Rue Royer-Collard, 75005 Paris

The bars and pubs around the Sorbonne are bustling with students taking breaks from their studies, many of whom enjoy sloshing back and forth between these two long-standing favorites.

For students who appreciate the extended happy hours, never-changing decor, and a list of over 300 cocktails, Le Crocodile is the spot. Just across the way is the cheap and cheerful Le Pantalon, with generally friendly service, shooters, and decent beers.

6th & 7th Arrondissements
Saint Germain / Invalides

Home of the Eiffel Tower, this is one of the city's most expensive areas, with upscale restaurants, chichi shopping, historic sensibilities, and well-heeled habitués. The bars follow suit with an appropriate level of quality and heritage.

17th

16th

7

15th

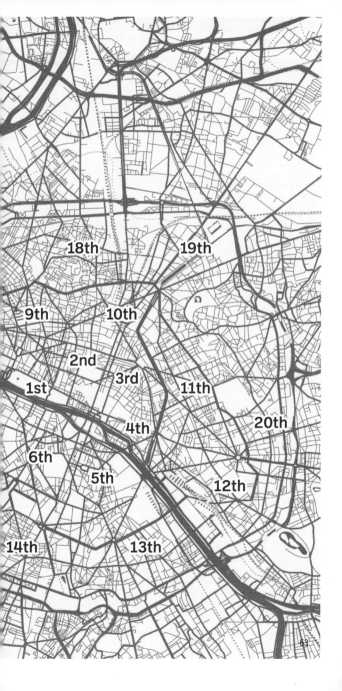

CASTOR CLUB

14 Rue Hautefeuille, 75006 Paris

You won't find Castor Club splashed around loads of blogs, travel reports, or listicles, yet somehow Parisian insiders seem to be intimately familiar with this discrete drinks venue. This is the address you keep hidden in your back pocket to pull out at just the right moment to confirm your nightlife cred and impress your drinking partner or date. (Although, with its intimate atmosphere and friendly bar staff, it also works well for a solo drink at the bar.)

The entirely unmarked door is tucked away in the chichi Saint-Germain-des-Prés neighborhood, through which confidently cool Parisians pass into a surreal little space. The decor applies Lynchian elements to a mountain cabin lodge for a stylish Scandi feel. Quirky lampshades decorated with exotic animals and jewel-tone velour stools and booths pop against the unfinished wooden-slat walls. A stuffed beaver on display references the bar's name—*castor* is the French word for this overgrown aquatic rodent. It's dim, dark, warm, and with a sort of sex appeal that is disconcertingly comforting, as is the soundtrack, which basically stops at midtwentieth-century tunes.

The bar staff flexes and stretches in the usual ways with shrubs and other bespoke ingredients. The signature cocktail, Chirac 95, is made with French ingredients, Calvados and Génépi, and recalls its namesake's first presidential victory. You can also go off the menu for classics or grab one of the beers, wines, or bubbles on offer by the glass.

And while the location remains somewhat confidential and discreet, enough of the cool crowd is in the loop to really pack it out during peak hours: late evening and weekends. To avoid too many people or the occasional gruff bouncer, go early evening or midweek when it's easier to score a seat at the small ground-floor bar. On busy nights and weekends, DJs entertain drinkers and dancers in the eighteenth century stone basement, complete with cozy wall nooks in which to canoodle.

Castor is one of those places that feels both completely foreign but also so, so French. No one talks about it, but everyone simply knows that it's the right place to go.

LA ROBE &
LA MOUSSE

3 Rue Monsieur le Prince, 75006 Paris

La Robe & La Mousse attracts a small but mighty contingent of local craft beer connoisseurs for its 100 percent French artisanal brews and other domestic drinks.

While Paris may have been a little late to the craft beer movement, they've been catching up swiftly over the last decade, reviving forgotten Parisian recipes and creating new flavor profiles. La Robe & La Mousse is an outpost of La Fine Mousse, an influential early champion of the artisanal beer trend in France and a regular favorite of local beer lovers. They are known for their impressive selection of quality beers from around the world.

What differentiates this second venue, La Robe & La Mousse, is its made-in-France policy. In addition to domestic beer, they offer other quality French alcoholic drinks like cider, mead, and natural wine. You'll find old-school options like the classic Salers gentian liqueur or the always popular Citadelle gin. But beer does remain the central focus at this happily hoppy taproom. And don't expect cocktail options. When spirits are served it's often neat and as an accompaniment to a good beer. They are also pretty good about keeping their online beer menu up to date via the untappd.com platform.

Basically, La Robe & La Mousse is a relaxed neighborhood bar where a cool French crowd goes for an easy apero hour without a lot of faff. Small plates and snacks are local as well, like French charcuterie or savory snack crackers.

Even the design is appealing, from its cheery turquoise shopfront to a warm interior where soft white neon pops against the deep blue walls. And the wooden bar, crafted with a true sense of style, is worth checking out.

Though located in an area of upscale restaurants, bars, and shops that have the potential to attract the pretentious, the beer crowd helps to keep it real here. The staff is friendly and seems sincerely happy to help clients work through the many draught and bottled options and often offer small tastes on request to facilitate decision making. It's really a pleasure to find the high-quality products that this neighborhood bar commands served with a genuine smile.

FITZGERALD

54 Bd de la Tour-Maubourg, 75007 Paris

Fitzgerald is a speakeasy hidden within a chic, seasonal restaurant of the same name, and it is the perfect expression of Left Bank insider cool.

It's not always easy to find good fare within a short walking distance of the Eiffel Tower, but this is an address worth having if you're in the area—and even worth occasionally crossing the Seine for. Although close to one of the city's biggest tourist attractions, Fitzgerald is on a relatively quiet street that caters almost exclusively to the residents. It draws in stylish locals who come for lunch or dinner but stay later when they discover the hush-hush bar hidden behind the unmarked large double door at the back of the room.

This small bar is inspired by a bygone era of bathtub gin and festive champagne coups. It's the sexy version of the secret gin joints of the 1920s, minus the life-threateningly bad homemade spirits and specter of arrest. And unlike some of the city's more notable cocktail bars on the Right Bank, here, you don't have the fuss of lines or doormen to break the spell of imaginary illicitness. No, this is simply a sophisticated place for grown-ups to enjoy a cocktail garnished with the romance of yesteryear.

The lights are dim and the decor is an elegant modern take on older times with flamingo wallpaper and comfy velour sofas, chairs, and stools in blue, gold, and orange tones. Look up and appreciate the vintage touch of the tin ceiling. It's all class.

Cocktails are creative and incorporate interesting flavors without being too over the top for this somewhat staid street; think tonka beans or rooibos tea. They also have a nice selection of nonalcoholic cocktails..

Prices are appropriate for a more mature audience, hovering a little higher than average. But that's the price of a location with an exclusive feel yet accessible entry.

As a bonus, the food in the restaurant is outstanding, so it's easy to make a full evening of your visit with pre- or post-dinner drinks (or both!)

FITZGERALD

The eponymous cocktail from this Left Bank speakeasy style lounge is easy to make at home, especially if you prep the syrup ahead of time.

1⅓ oz. Tanqueray Gin

⅔ oz. fresh lemon juice

⅔ oz. Rosemary Syrup

10 dashes Angostura Bitters

Fever Tree Tonic Water, to top

1. Add all of the ingredients, except the tonic, to a tall glass, fill with ice, and top with the tonic.

2. Stir gently to mix but not enough to flatten the bubbles.

3. Garnish with a sprig of rosemary.

Rosemary Syrup: In a saucepan, combine 2 cups water, 2 cups sugar, and 1 cup rosemary honey and gently boil for 20 minutes. Add 3 or 4 rosemary sprigs, remove the pan from the heat, cover, and let stand for 6 hours. Strain the mixture and gently boil again for 10 minutes. Let cool and then refrigerate to store.

L'ECLAIR

32 Rue Cler, 75007 Paris

With friendly staff, fun drinks, and a cheerful disposition, this cute café and cocktail bar is designed to make you smile.

L'Eclair is not your typical Parisian café. It delivers a prettier and more polished experience. Situated on a cobblestone pedestrian street popular for its bakeries, boutiques, and florists, this sweet little spot is a creation of the Maison Boudon. This group has three other solid restaurant bars under its belt with La Fontaine de Mars, Le Petit Lutetia, and L'Alma. They know how to pack a place with personality and create fresh-faced, convivial spaces that adhere to their mission of "a daily life inspired by the savoir vivre of yesterday and our terroirs." In other words, establishments that retain a hint of history and aim for good service with quality local fare.

The place is just as popular for burgers and brunches as for its tiny cocktail bar. Outside of mealtime, shoppers and flaneurs sit on the terrace for a glass of wine with mixed plates of charcuterie and cheese. If you're feeling frisky, they also have some breezy cocktails to kick start your evening. In line with their easy-going vibe, the cocktails are less straight up and strong and more modern classic. You might enjoy a Porn Star Martini or the bright green Gin Basil Smash. Their team also creates its own playful cocktails with a range of spirits—again, lighthearted things that make you smile. The menu often features shareable drinks, like punch in pitchers, which further reinforces their efforts to make sure customers enjoy in a spirit of congeniality.

Prices may be a smidge higher for drinks and snacks than a standard café, but, as they say in France, it's "correct." This commonly used French descriptor means that the price-to-quality ratio is exactly right and you get what you pay for.

L'AVANT COMPTOIR DE LA TERRE

3 Carr de l'Odéon, 75006 Paris

When foodie friends say to me "I've only got one day in Paris, where should I go?" L'Avant Comptoir is my sure-fire suggestion. This pocket-size wine bar opened just over a decade ago next door to the Yves Camdeborde restaurant Le Comptoir as an overspill area for diners waiting for a table at this exceptional no-reservations restaurant.

L'Avant Comptoir is the classic victim of its own success in that it was so much fun it became a destination in its own right. The place is packed like sardines with locals ordering small producer and natural French wines to wash down meat-heavy snacks like oxtail croque monsieur or foie gras brochettes. Vegetarians, avert your eyes! Oh, and don't overlook the mound of beautifully bright yellow butter on the counter that is the size of your head.

The menu is a collection of laminated cards hanging from the ceiling that features the name, price, and photo of the food items on offer. A short list of wine is suggested on chalkboards but many more bottles line the shelves behind the bar, just begging guests to dive down a rabbit hole of worthwhile local options. The white tile walls are covered with Sharpie pen scribbles of random food-related graffiti like wineglasses or cartoon mer-pigs (that's a creature that's half pork, half fish) and more. There isn't really much in the way of seats or tables, so just squish in and order at the bar with the dozens of other jocular new "friends."

Prices are very reasonable, which is another reason for its popularity. It also spawned great little sister venues, L'Avant Comptoir de la Mer next door (with a focus on seafood) and the larger L'Avant Comptoir du Marche, a short walk away with a bit more indoor and outdoor seating and tables.

L'Avant Comptoir is a small but mighty must for any visitor looking to rub elbows and bump shoulders with the city's food and wine enthusiasts.

HOTEL DE L'ABBAYE

10 Rue Cassette, 75006 Paris

Hotel de l'Abbaye's bucolic hidden garden and sitting room bar is one of St. Germain's best-kept secrets.

Formerly a Benedictine convent, the Hotel de l'Abbaye is an boutique hotel with only 44 rooms. As such, it's relatively quiet. Which is how they like it. They don't actively advertise their secret garden and fireside salon and instead rely on word of mouth to attract those who will properly appreciate this confidential address. Thus, in-the-know locals confidently stroll in to enjoy a quiet, private drink in some of the city's most beautiful surroundings.

One of my many favorite things about this location is that it works so very well for all seasons. In the winter months, I head to the sitting room for the blazing fire. Because of the hotel's small stature, there is an intimacy to all the spaces, so this room feels like you've wandered into your well-off French friend's luxury apartment. Tasteful sofas are upholstered to match the heavy drapes, expensive and expansive paintings adorn the walls—this is definitely the kind of establishment in which walls are "adorned."

On cool spring or autumn days the glassed-in veranda is the perfect place to sit under blue skies and sunshine without a chill. It's a feminine room with stylish striped chairs, sofas punctuated by accent pillows, and roses on the tables. This is where you take your granny, your girlfriends, or your GBF for an afternoon drink.

The pièce de resistance? The garden terrace, surrounded by walls covered with ivy where the only sound you'll hear is the bubbling fountain. It's idyllic.

If the bartender is on hand, you can order up a martini or something off their cocktail menu. Otherwise, it's best to stick with bubbles, which are apropos for this elegant space. Whatever you order comes with upscale bar snacks and you can supplement them with something from the food menu, like a spring or winter salad or a croque monsieur.

BAR JOSEPHINE

45 Bd Raspail, 75006 Paris

Following a €200 million revamp in 2018, the iconic Hotel Lutetia is better than ever, and if you can't afford one of the rooms, at least you can live some of the legend in their beautiful Bar Josephine.

This stunning art nouveau building has played a significant role in Parisian history. Since its opening in 1910 by founders of the major French department store Le Bon Marché, celebrated personalities like Picasso and James Joyce have raised glasses here. Of course, its namesake, Josephine Baker, also passed through on occasion. It was even requisitioned by the Nazis during World War II.

The first thing you notice about Bar Josephine is the sheer size. Ceilings are high and the room is wide, and this expanse is further accentuated by the large amount of light coming in through the windows that run along the front of the building. This also makes it all that much easier to appreciate the impressive floor-to-ceiling frescos covering all the walls.

The cocktails play with unusual ingredients and flavors like bamboo, shiitake, and vinegar. But in a place like this you could easily go for a classic, which will likely come with an extra special touch, like a few truffled cocktail onions alongside a martini. But this menu is more than just cocktails. There is a small well-curated list of wines by the glass followed by pages and pages of spirits, with dozens of choices in each category. This is where you want to treat yourself to a more unusual whisky or taste of a quality saké.

Not surprisingly in a hotel of this level, prices are above average, which accounts for the attention to detail. Polite staff bring bottomless dishes of fancy nuts and olives. However, with so much ground to cover, service can take a little longer than average. So, go with a relaxed attitude, the kind which only the luxury of not being in a rush can bring.

Another extra that makes drinks here worth the price is the Thursday through Saturday live jazz.

LA CLOSERIE DES LILAS

171 Bd du Montparnasse, 75006 Paris

Ernest Hemingway frequented the bar of this historic brasserie, which still smolders in the embers of old-world Parisian charm with nightly piano music and stiff martinis.

Opened in 1847, this legendary location has always drawn those with an artistic bent. Over the years the likes of Verlaine, Baudelaire, Henry Miller, Picasso, Gertrude Stein, Tim Burton, and Johnny Depp have passed through. Hemingway wrote large parts of *The Sun Also Rises* here and mentions it by name in *A Moveable Feast*. Today, his usual table is indicated with a little brass nameplate.

But unlike some of the other Montparnasse haunts popular on the Lost Generation drinking circuit, La Closerie's bar still does a pretty consistently bang-up job. Avuncular barmen in crisp whites stir up classics or shake up creations and ceremoniously serve them on sweet little branded paper coasters. (Shhhh: so cute, I've been known to nick a few!) Drinks come with bowls of briny olives or homemade potato chips. I prefer sitting right at the tiny zinc bar, but the beautiful red vinyl booths near the musicians also have their appeal.

This bar doesn't garner the same global attention as some of the city's other historic heavyweights, like Les Deux Magots, which seems to figure more frequently in guides and lists. And maybe that's why you still get a good mix of locals coming through. On a recent visit, to my left at the bar was a jolly duo of tourists but to my right was a famous French actor. As a local, I go there for early birthday drinks, when playing tour guide, or most recently simply for a solo cocktail while listening to the piano player. I've also been for drinks followed by dinner on the big busy terrace and, while not a destination restaurant, the food is typical brasserie fare and delightfully acceptable in a pinch.

If a similar bar were created elsewhere in Paris with the same beautiful art deco design, old-school barmen stirring decent drinks, and a talented musician tickling the ivories, it would still lack the mythic history that defines La Closerie des Lilas.

LE SELECT

99 Bd du Montparnasse, 75006 Paris

A glimmer of Montparnasse's heady heyday lives on in the unassuming Le Select café.

There is no better place to chase the city's 1920s' literary and artistic past than on this one-block stretch of Boulevard Montparnasse, where you'll find four cafés often mentioned in the same breath as F. Scott Fitzgerald, Picasso, Ernest Hemingway, Man Ray, and Kiki de Montparnasse. All of these café brasseries are significant in their own way, but the least opulent of them all, Le Select, holds a special place in the hearts of many. Hemingway is said to have called it "the soul of Montmartre."

While the other three may be grander, Le Select is a little less showy. Yet it still has everything you want in a traditional brasserie: classic bistro chairs, a big terrace, a beautifully tiled floor, and art deco design elements. And maybe that's what draws the locals. You go to the other three to be wowed like a tourist. You come to Le Select simply to drink *comme il faut*.

While the standard French food here is so-so, this is the best of the four for a drink. Depending on the time of day or year, the others may not have space at their tiny bars or much, if any, outside seating open. Here, locals fill the large sidewalk terrace where they order glasses of wine and beer and consume endless little dishes of olives and nuts. They might even splash out on a tasty plate of charcuterie. On sunny afternoons, bigger groups order bottles of white wine that professional waitstaff set up in silver ice buckets next to the white cloth-covered tables. It's also the best of the big cafés for martinis, which are relatively consistent.

Le Select wavered little over the decades and continued to draw the city's writers. James Baldwin worked on *Giovanni's Room* here and even mentions it by name in the book.

Today, sitting on the sidewalk terrace of Le Select you'll still occasionally see eager young écrivains cracking open fresh notebooks. And thus, the Parisian literary legend and myth lives on at Le Select.

Favorite Spot for Daytime Drinking

TREIZE AU JARDIN
5 Rue de Médicis, 75006 Paris

Don't miss the charming spot, just across the street from the Luxembourg Gardens. This bakery, coffee shop, and teahouse has a fab selection of wine and cocktails, including a G&T in a teapot.

More Left Bank Favorites

TIGER
13 Rue Princesse, 75006 Paris

FREDDY'S
54 Rue de Seine, 75006 Paris

PRESCRIPTION COCKTAIL CLUB
23 Rue Mazarine, 75006 Paris

Start your night with a pre-dinner G&T at the city's only dedicated gin bar, Tiger. From there, head to Freddy's, a wine bar where you can make a light dinner out of their exceptional small plates paired with a glass of red or white. Finish up with a nightcap at Prescription Cocktail Club.

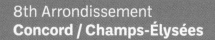

8th Arrondissement
Concord / Champs-Élysées

This is Paris at its finest, with fashionable designer boutiques, four-star hotels, and historic landmarks. Here you'll find the most expensive and high-end style of bars that fit right into the area's upper-class lifestyle.

17th

16th

7t

15th

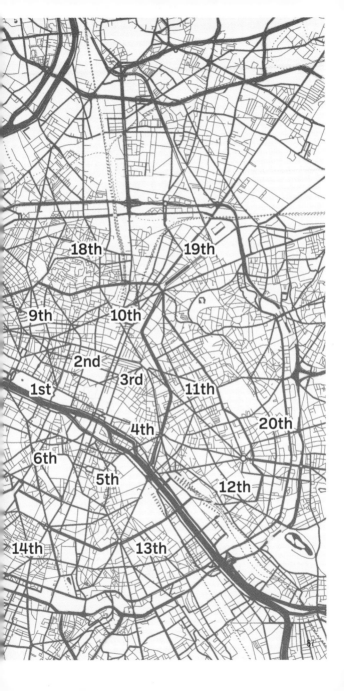

LE BAR FOUR SEASONS GEORGE V

31 Av. George V, 75008 Paris

With its Louis XVI decor and a palace-worthy drinks menu, Le Bar is among the crème de la crème of Paris hotel bars.

In France, there's a level of accommodation even more distinguished than a five-star hotel: the "Palace." Establishments achieve "Distinction Palace" by going above and beyond in all areas of their property and hospitality. Built nearly a century ago, the Four Seasons George V is an art deco landmark that—at the time of writing— boasts three Michelin-starred restaurants and luxurious rooms starting at around two grand a night. At those prices, the closest I get to reveling in this level of luxury is an evening in their gorgeous Le Bar.

Le Bar is where the rich and famous hotel guests drop after they shop at nearby Chanel, Hermès, and Louis Vuitton. But, it's also where Parisians who know how and where to treat themselves to real luxury go to celebrate a special milestone or carry out a classy rendezvous.

The selection of wine is impressive and something sparkling is so fitting in these surroundings. But they also deliver with their cocktail program. The menu includes both creations and George V takes on classics like the Old Fashioned, Negroni, and Spritz. Bar snacks are classy and range from lobster rolls to high-roller caviar service.

It's fitting that this hotel has the palace distinction, because it feels as decadent as an evening at Versaille. The chandeliers twinkle, the classic wood bar gleams, and the lamps cast a warm and flattering glow over guests. Fresh flowers stand in tall vases on the bar and in small centerpieces on the tables.

While Paris currently has around a dozen palace hotels, not all high-end hotel bars in Paris are created equally. So, it's nice to know when you are about to drop at least $30 on a cocktail that the experience will be worth it. At George V Le Bar, it will be.

LES AMBASSADEURS

10 Pl. de la Concorde, 75008 Paris

Ever wonder what it would be like to go back to the eighteenth century and drink with French royals? Les Ambassadeurs bar in the Crillon hotel is your time machine to a private residence commissioned by Louis XV in 1758. It's a historical venue but with a welcome contemporary twist since you can make this time travel with a cocktail in hand.

A few years back this iconic hotel closed for four years for a complete renovation. The result is an establishment that keeps the vestiges of its royal heritage but also has a modern-day polish.

The neoclassical Crillon faces the legendary Place de la Concorde and is also right next to the American embassy. That means you get a good mix of curious tourists, swanky hotel guests, visiting diplomats, and high-level American expats.

In keeping with the location and level of clientele, this is the place you go to for cocktails, champagne, or caviar. The wine list is extensive and cocktails include both revisited classics and house creations.

The decor is eye-poppingly opulent with gilding, mirrors, chandeliers, ceiling frescos, and a beautiful rounded freestanding bar. This is also the type of place that doesn't skimp on presentation so expect beautiful stemware and stamped ice cubes. They also enforce a casual chic dress code.

Of course, the drinks are pricey. But extra bonuses make up for the extra cost. A resident orchestra plays soul, jazz, hip-hop, and more several nights a week; keep an eye on the website for the musical lineup so you can sink into one of the comfortable armchairs and enjoy some sounds and sips.

In the words of the Crillon management: "The building has stood through the reigns of two French kings, the French Revolution, the rise and fall of the Napoleonic Empire, and the birth of the League of Nations." That's a lot of history to drink in.

GENTLEMEN 1919

11 Rue Jean Mermoz, 75008 Paris

Gentlemen 1919 is a speakeasy and *fumoir* hidden behind a barbershop, making it a one-stop shop for a haircut, cigar, and a drink.

The red-and-white barber's pole spins in front of what seems like a standard hip salon. Head inside past the stylists and confidently open the unmarked door in the back to discover a gentlemen's (and gentlewomen's!) club, complete with leather chesterfields and a separate smoking room.

Gentlemen 1919 embodies a bygone era with its nostalgic decor of leather, brick, and wood. Even the name recalls a more illicit chapter of alcohol's history; 1919 is the year that Prohibition began in the United States. While speakeasies ironically seem to get the most press, this one stays relatively quiet on the international circuit so you get a lot of locals appreciating the yesteryear vibes. However, it is in one of the city's more affluent arrondissements, so you also get a handful of tourists who follow the recommendations of their trusty concierges at high-end hotels. The swanky postal code and exclusive atmosphere also mean that prices hover a little higher than average for drinks.

You can enjoy cocktails named after gangsters like Al Capone's Scarface or the Sam Giancana inspired Cigar for Sam. Classics are also handled with care and a martini or Old Fashioned would not be out of place. But, it's also the kind of venue where you feel at home with a neat whisky. Or if you get to know the regulars, you might get a sip of something special from bottles they store in private onsite rented lockers.

The bar is open during the day and you can even get a little nip of something strong to sip while getting your hair styled. It's possible to reserve online for the bar, which I highly recommend for evenings since it's a small space that the cool crowd is already clued into. And to make it even classier, you can also get your leather treated or shoes shined here.

In short: it's everything you need to be a snappy, well-coiffed, modern-day scofflaw!

GENTLEMEN 1919 SOUR

This egg white sour is the perfect choice for the speakeasy's eponymous cocktail, reflecting its both sharp and silky style.

½ egg white or ½ tbsp. aquafaba

1½ oz. bourbon

½ oz. tequila

⅓ oz. fresh lemon juice

⅔ oz. fig syrup

1. Add the egg white or aquafaba to a shaker and dry shake for 10 seconds.

2. Add the remaining ingredients to the shaker, fill halfway with ice, and shake energetically for 10 to 15 seconds.

3. Strain into a rocks glass over ice and, if desired, garnish with edible flowers.

DRINKS&CO

106 bis Rue Saint-Lazare, 75008 Paris

What looks like a busy bottle shop just steps from the high-traffic area of the Saint-Lazare train station is also a very lively bar.

This large space is so much more than just a boozy boutique. Drinks&Co is a spirits shop, bar, restaurant, and event space for workshops around alcohol, wine, cocktails, and nonalcoholic drinks. And while you can settle onto a stool at the wooden counter that runs the length of the front room any time, things really start hopping as the evening draws closer.

Around 7 p. m., the lights get slightly dimmed and all of the tables and barstools and the terrace space are full of locals catching up over afterwork drinks. Conversation is animated and carried out over the sound of shakers. Shoppers perusing the shelves, chatting with staff, and making purchases add to the energetic ambience.

It's not just a unique space to drink, but also a good place to find a liquid souvenir. It's easy to find something unusual as the shop stocks some 1,200 different products. About 50 percent of the large inventory is domestic and also includes interesting niche products. Bottled cocktails are available to go, which makes a fun alternative to wine for a picnic or a nice nightcap in a hotel room.

All of this takes place in a chic space, from the snappy blue awnings outside to the big, bold, organic graphics that cover the walls and tree trunk—like columns. The layout invites circulation, making it easy to move around the tables and the well-stocked shelves. A separate freestanding bar is set up in a backroom to make space for the master classes.

This hybrid concept adds an extra fun element to both shopping and sipping cocktails, the staff is very welcoming and accommodating, and there is a strong focus on nonalcoholic cocktails making this a

great destination even for families. With all that, it's surprising more tourists have yet to discover Drinks&Co. The current crowd remains mostly French, with a wide range of locals from young happy hipsters to more mature, experienced barhoppers.

RAS 'N' ROLL

Drinks&Co's Mirror menu features cocktails with their alcohol-free counterparts that still express the same spirit, like this one. Nonalcoholic ingredients follow the alcoholic ones.

1⅔ oz. Apérol or Lyre's Italian Spritz

3 oz. Rhubarb & Ras el Hanout Cordial

4 drops Stillabunt Velvet Magic Foamer or Fee Brothers Fee Foam

1 pinch sea salt

1. Combine all of the ingredients in a cocktail shaker and dry shake for 10 seconds.
2. Fill the shaker halfway with ice, shake energetically for 10 to 15 seconds, and strain into a chilled highball or champagne flute over ice.
3. Stir slightly and enjoy.

Rhubarb and Ras el Hanout Cordial: Slice a fresh stalk of rhubarb into small pieces, add the sliced rhubarb to a glass jar, cover it with sugar, and muddle. Cover and let stand for two days until the sugar has dissolved. Strain the mixture into a saucepan and combine it with two parts filtered water. Add a little less than a teaspoon of ras el hanout for each cup of liquid and then gently heat the liquid to 140°F, maintaining that temperature for 1 hour. Strain through a coffee filter—lined fine mesh sieve and refrigerate to store.

9th Arrondissement
Pigalle / Rue des Martyrs

This edgily cool area includes both the city's old red-light district and one of its most iconic foodie streets for a mix of high- and lowbrow. Some of the best places to drink like a local around here mirror that with quality drinks consumed in venues that aren't afraid to show a bit cheek.

17th

16th

7

15th

CLASSIQUE

1bis Rue Lallier, 75009 Paris

Classique plays on its location, originally a nine-teenth-century pharmacy, maintaining a charming French apothecary aesthetic. They've even kept the classic green cross signage that traditionally identifies French drugstores.

When I ask fellow drinks writers in France about favorite spots, Classique is a name that often comes up. And there is a lot to like about this little place.

The decor is stylish with retro touches like the old floor tiles that recall its past, but the overall interior design is polished enough to feel contemporary. Well-worn dark wooden stools are dotted around the marble bar and the booth seating around the tables is classic. Lots of light and wood trim against white and cream walls give it a clean and elegant feel. It's an interior space for people with good taste.

However, it's not all about what's on the inside here. Their location on a sort of thin pointed corner gives them a lot of front sidewalk area, where they put out plenty of bistro chairs and tables for a sizable terrace. Sidewalk sipping is a big part of French culture, so when the weather is warm plenty of fun young residents of this hip neighborhood settle in with trendy IPAs or coffee.

While the cocktail menu includes less common flavors like pandan and umeshu, they work the ingredients in a way to ensure a collection of well-balanced cocktails. Classique is the kind of bar where they make many of their own ingredients, which often line the counter or shelves in unmarked vials and bottles and add to the pharmaceutical vibe. The Champagne is Natur, an on-trend option that means no extra sugar is added. Coffee is a house blend.

The food menu completes the package with quality small plates like burrata or king crab rolls (not something you find often in France). They also have an oyster happy hour with specials on bivalves and cocktails or a bottle of wine.

With its strong combo of design, drinks, and food, Classique is the kind of place you'll spot on the Instagram feeds of tastemakers and trendsetters.

ERBALUNGA

This signature cocktail from Classique is named after a little village on the French island of Corsica, which is where its main ingredient is made.

2 oz. Cap Mattei Grande Réserve

⅘ oz. fresh lime juice

½ oz. Maple & Tonka Syrup

½ oz. Lapsang Cordial

1. Combine all of the ingredients in a cocktail shaker with ice, shake well for 15 to 20 seconds, and double strain into a chilled cocktail glass.

Maple & Tonka Syrup: In a saucepan, combine two parts maple syrup to one part filtered water. Grate tonka beans over the mixture, to taste, then bring the mixture to a boil. When it begins to boil, remove the pan from the heat and let stand for 30 minutes before straining into a bottle. Refrigerate to store.

Lapsang Cordial: In a container with a lid, combine 4 teaspoons red fruit tea, 1 teaspoon loose lapsang souchong tea, and 1 cup water and refrigerate for 6 hours. Strain into a bottle, add 2 oz. agave syrup, shake well, and refrigerate to store.

SISTER MIDNIGHT

4 Rue Viollet le-Duc, 75009 Paris

Sister Midnight is reintroducing to the city some of Pigalle's bygone gritty chic with ice-cold cocktails and saucy entertainment.

Even though it's on a somewhat quiet side street of the neighborhood now nicknamed SoPi (South of Pigalle), you won't miss it thanks to the unapologetically hot pink name scrawled across the dark awning. Inside, it's a low-lit and sexy boudoir vibe with fringe-trimmed lampshades (made by co-owner Jen), deep blue walls, and leopard print accents. The disco ball and mirrored ceiling whisper 1970s' trash glam, which is an integral part of this edgy establishment's ethos. The small space provides an intimacy that makes it easy to slide onto a stool at the shiny black bar and strike up a conversation with the friendly staff.

With impressive cocktail credentials, the team here can stir up a spot-on classic. I've certainly ordered my fair share of martinis here. But don't overlook the regularly changing cocktail menu, which highlights a handful of their creations and includes everything from easy-going drinks to more challenging cocktails, like the dark black, chipotle-spiked Suicide.

On Sundays, their five-martini menu is available with options from the relatively classic Oyster Martini to their totally interesting take on the espresso martini that uses

Vietnamese iced *cà phê*. Of course, there are beers on tap, craft brews by the bottle, and various bubbles.

A small food menu makes it easy to belly up to the bar for longer with snacks like anchovy-stuffed tarragon olives or a more substantial ploughman's platter of cheese, chutney, and pickled egg.

But Sister Midnight is best known for the weekly drag burlesque and cabaret shows that have not only gained quite the reputation, but sassily wink to the area's previous position as Paris's red-light district. A regular rotation of local talent sashays through on high heels to vamp up and amp up the ambience. Be prepared for big crowds on these nights. But if you want something a little more laid-back, go early in the evening when you can reserve up until 9 p.m. Either way it's a definite detour from the typical tourist trail.

RUBY TUESDAY

This light and fruity little number is a fresh twist on the omnipresent Negroni.

1 oz. Blueberry Gin

½ oz. Italian-style bitters (preferably Berto or Dolin)

½ oz. Dubonnet

1 tsp. Cointreau

Lemon zest

1. Build the drink in a double rocks glass over ice. Stir, express the lemon zest over the drink, and then drop it into the glass.

Blueberry Gin: In a large container with a lid, muddle 1 cup blueberries. Add 1 bottle of gin (and reserve the bottle). Cover and let stand for 24 hours. Strain and store in the reserved bottle.

DIRTY DICK

10 Rue Frochot, 75009 Paris

Dirty Dick differentiated itself by being the first tiki bar to set up shop in Paris. But they don't just rely on their unique position as the only such bar in town to stay relevant. They pull out all the stops to deliver tropical vibes and top-notch rum-based libations.

This well-known watering hole is located in SoPi, which was formerly the city's red-light district. The bar took over what was previously a strip club and entirely changed the type of entertainment found in this establishment, but retained the name.

Here, you'll find typical tiki touches like statement wallpaper, wooden masks, rattan and bamboo barstools, plus a few items that dial this decor up to eleven, like the two huge custom-carved totem poles and the bikini babe mural by American artist David "Gonzo" Gonzalez. And the restrooms don't escape the tropical treatment with a soundtrack of chirping birdies.

It's not just the decor that does it right here, but the drinks too. There is a notably large selection of rums and rum-based drinks. Ingredients are prepped in house with TLC. Glassware includes custom ceramic mugs made by local artist Baï. Much like tiki, it's both kitsch and class; a bit of good escapist fun but with a serious foundation of solid recipes and know-how.

This is the kind of place you go for a convivial punch bowl with friends or solo to meet and mingle with the locals. Going along with its good times vibe, the bar is open every day and nestled amongst plenty of other popular SoPi spots so it's easy to make a rowdy night of it. Dirty Dick is a tropical dive bar, hipster hideout, and excellent cocktail lounge all rolled into one where young and lively locals pack the place out from early evening. Lights are dim—all the better to watch the fruit-filled drinks set aflame. And it's the kind of place that stays open a little later on the weekends.

MAISON SOUQUET

10 Rue de Bruxelles, 75009 Paris

The Pigalle neighborhood is well-known for its racy red-light past and many of its old bordellos have been repurposed into cocktail lounges or boudoir-style bars in the now trendy SoPi neighborhood. And while exotic sex shows and erotic toy shops can still be found here, most of the locals are heading this way to satisfy their cocktail rather than carnal cravings in classy bars that celebrate the city's belle époque past like that of the Maison Souquet. Just steps away from the Moulin Rouge, this five-star hotel is housed in what was once a brothel and still makes lighthearted reference to its steamy past with the cocktail names and paintings on the walls.

The low-key entrance to this boutique hotel is marked by two red lamps and transports you to a dreamy Moorish-inspired lobby. Keep going through to the sexy little bar and you'll find yourself in a dim, quiet room that's all dark wood and deep crimson velour: a welcome respite for the modern-day coquette. The large fireplace gives an impression of warmth even if not lit, and chess and other cerebral games are available for guests. A second small room is more frilly, with floral sofas, comfy armchairs, and large mirrors that reflect twinkling lamplight. Just beyond this second room is a tiny terrace with one bench overlooking a garden statue—just big enough to seat two lovebirds. All of this recalls the location's artistic past and its former status as a brothel.

While its past may be steamy, this hotel commands higher prices for cocktails and has a basement swimming pool that can be privatized by guests. And, being in a hotel, of course, it pulls in its fair share of visiting guests. But, it's also a confidential hideaway for locals seeking a discreet address for date nights and romantic rendezvous.

More Fun Bars in the 9th

HOTEL AMOUR
8 Rue de Navarin 75009 Paris

NO ENTRY
20 bis Rue de Douai, 75009 Paris

LE MANSART
1 Rue Mansart, 75009 Paris

COQ AND BULLDOG
64 Rue de Clichy, 75009 Paris

Head to the secret garden terrace of Hotel Amour, the No Entry speakeasy hidden in a popular pizzeria, the lively Le Mansart for fun on the terrace with a young carefree crowd, or the Coq and Bulldog, a tiny and truly welcoming pub that pulls in all the neighborhood residents.

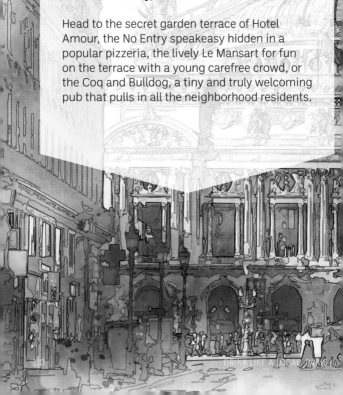

10th Arrondissement
Strasbourg-Saint-Denis /
Canal Saint-Martin

This diverse and historically working-class area is not yet fully gentrified so pockets of affordable rent attract hip, young Parisians. The bars reflect a similar youthfully up-to-date sensibility with cool cocktail bars and lively terraces that make life feel like a party.

17th

16th

7t

15th

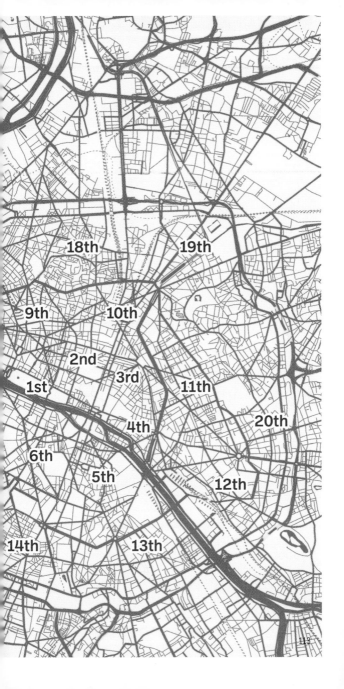

18th

19th

9th

10th

2nd

3rd

1st

11th

4th

20th

6th

5th

12th

14th

13th

113

DELAVILLE CAFÉ

34-36 Bd de Bonne Nouvelle, 75010 Paris

This Parisian institution offers a little something for everyone with an expansive sunny terrace and an opulent interior that was originally a nineteenth-century bordello in Napoleon's Paris.

You won't escape hearing English at this popular café. A terrace this size does not go unnoticed by strolling tourists needing a break from all the sightseeing. But, it also draws a loyal legion of chic young Parisians. It's rumored to be a meeting point for quasi-famous French actors and children of celebs, though I haven't seen (or recognized) any there.

What's behind the terrace is definitely worth the price of a drink. Its prior incarnations include brothel, upscale belle époque dining establishment, and Chinese restaurant. Though the centuries have subdued its opulence, you still get a gander at grander historical times throughout the multiple rooms and different levels of its restaurant, bar, and drinking areas. Large mirrors hang in high-ceilinged rooms. A stunning marble and iron staircase is hidden off the side of the restaurant. Seats are upholstered in burgundy and red velour.

Like many of the city's destination terraces, Delaville is often more about the al fresco element than serious cocktails; the bartenders generally tweak up the sweetness levels to please a younger palate. Fortunately, there's always the possibility of finding a very drinkable beer or wine on most French menus. And really, this is the kind of place that's perfect for people watching with a cheap and cheerful bottle of rosé.

Delaville is open seven days a week from early morning to late at night. However, different times have distinctly different moods. Early birds take a quieter coffee in the morning sun—or brunch on the weekends. Come noon, hungry patrons order standard dishes from classic French *oeufs mayos* to the popular burger. Early evening gets things hopping with a happy hour that runs extra long on Sundays and Mondays. Late nights turn into more of a party atmosphere when DJs spin on weekends.

CAFÉ A

148 Rue du Faubourg Saint-Martin, 75010 Paris

The garden terrace of this popular restaurant and events space inside the Maison de l'Architecture is cloistered away from the busy street and nearby hectic train station by an old stone wall, providing welcome tranquility.

The complex was initially a convent commissioned by Henri IV, which eventually became a military hospital. After a few wars and many years of use, it fell into a state of disrepair that led to its closure in 1968.

Fortunately, it was renovated and reopened this century to become an HQ for thirtysomethings looking for a little escape from the city. On the terrace, canvas sun loungers are scattered around the walled garden and green leafy trees sway a little lazily in the breeze. Off-white pebble ground cover reflects the sunlight. Its uniqueness makes it a favorite of Parisians to meet friends for an aperitif of a biodynamic wine or even just a sparkling water.

Another big draw is their events program. You might find yourself in a winter ski chalet setup with faux fur thrown over the garden furniture and gondola cars strategically placed around pop-up bars. Another time it may be a Cuban-inspired week of sunny summer fun with specialty rum drinks. Other events involve local artists, film screenings, DJs, or gardening workshops. Basically, between the terrace garden, organized activities, and the restaurant you can make a full day and evening here.

Although the prices are higher than the average café in this working-class neighborhood, the eco-friendly, artistic bent of the events calls to creative and bohemian types who have quickly made this a regular end-of-day drinks destination. And being a little hidden from public view means it's less obvious to tourists. Only locals know to push through the gate and cross the courtyard to access the hidden haven. They also know to go in the afternoon or early evening to secure a seat because it's usually a full house by sundown.

CHEZ JEANNETTE

47 Rue du Faubourg Saint-Denis, 75010 Paris

Chez Jeanette is a right of passage for young Parisians, discovering its grungy cool decor that was put in place before they were born. When its name comes up, those over thirty are likely to look a bit nostalgic and say, "Yes! Chez Jeanette! I haven't been for years..." But there's always a new crop of young barhoppers who congregate on the little terrace or slide into red booths to soak in a vintage vibe with good friends and new acquaintances.

This popular café bar has always been a neighborhood watering hole and doesn't really strive to be anything more. It's named after the former owner, who sold it in 2007 with the caveat that nothing be changed, including the name. It's a little bit dusty and a little bit divey. The floor and counter are scuffed and the walls have yellowed with time, but it only seems to add a patina that recalls past decades.

The animated conversations and rock music get louder as the evening wears on and the fluorescent lights dim. They also serve standard food, including burgers, which are popular with hungry regulars. But this isn't where you go for the pinnacle of French dining, so a plate of charcuterie is a safer bet.

The best way to soak in Chez Jeanette is to go before it gets too busy and score a seat by the large windows to watch the students, fashion victims, and neighborhood habitués who traipse through.

Sometimes the service is good. More often less so. But, to many, that's just part of the "charm." It's surely seen better days, but in an area that is rapidly gentrifying with new cocktail bars and trendy eateries, there's something comforting about the fact that this spot seems to stay the same. And there is much to be said for inexpensive small glasses of wine and pints of beer.

LE COMPTOIR GENERALE

84 Quai de Jemmapes, 75010 Paris

You go to the bar of this curio-filled large multipurpose venue built in a former barn for more than a drink. You go for the experience.

The entrance is hidden behind a wall on Canal Saint-Martin, where a long corridor lit by old chandeliers and lined with a long red carpet leads to a space that is bar, restaurant, bric-a-brac shop, cinema, coffeehouse, greenhouse, and collector's gallery all rolled into one. It's hard to take everything in all at once, so your eyes just dart from vintage typewriters to taxidermy birds. The collection includes both cultural and natural artifacts from all over the world.

Their "pirate boat bar" doesn't escape the eclectic makeover either. It looks like the bow of a ship sailing into the center of a large industrial room hung with garlands of colorful pennants and stringed lights. There is also a lot to look at on the drink menu, including some options that are less familiar for the French like kombucha. Of course, they have a decent selection of wine, domestic beer, champagne, signature cocktails, and a dedicated section for rum drinks, which helps cultivate the sense of Caribbean escapism the bar is going for. Finally, they offer a couple of G&T combinations with fancy tonics and more unusual gin. And, though the quality of the cocktails can be a little fluid depending on how busy it gets, there's definitely enough to work with.

Le Comptoir brings in a strolling saxophonist on certain evenings who meanders through the different dreamlike scenes to accompany their carefully curated playlist looping in the background. Other times DJs spin later in the evening.

You get a mixture of locals here from hip bourgeois-bo-hemians to harried parents coming for brunch. Le Comptoir is often referred to as "off-the-beaten path." And that it is, but it's still a well-trodden path. That becomes especially clear when you arrive late to find long lines. But it's still worth a detour for the experience and maybe a rare souvenir, so head there early to avoid a wait.

COPPERBAY

5 Rue Bouchardon, 75010 Paris

CopperBay does some heavy lifting when it comes to introducing the wider Parisian public to quality cocktails. Owners Elfi, Aurélie, and Julien have serious cocktail cred and have put heart and soul into this place, which shines when it comes to democratizing mixed drinks and delivering something that's equally well received by mixology newbies and experienced cocktail quaffers.

This Mediterranean-inspired bar was one of the early Paris cocktail spots to make a determined detour from the dark and hidden speakeasy style that had become so popular. They lightened up with a marine-inspired decor of blond wood, shiny copper, and arresting blue, all visible through the large street-front windows. Bar and table seating are consistently full in the front, and the back of the bar offers up a square booth area that's somewhat removed, making it a great option for small groups to catch up.

No detail goes overlooked and that includes the regularly changing menu, though the staff has the chops to work off the menu if you need a classic dry martini, which you can order with their eponymous house navy strength or regular gin created in collaboration with the Distillerie de Paris. Or get inspired by the team's penchant for pastis, and make like you are hanging at the port of Marseille with a glass or a carafe of this southern standby. Try their Pastis Mauresco collaboration created with Marseille-based la Distillerie de la Plaine (also available for purchase by the bottle).

In addition to cocktails, they offer a small list of natural wines, French beer, and a few options for bubbles. The food menu includes tasty snacks like the meze plate

with hummus, tarama, and tirokafteri or their exclusive pastis hake rillettes created in collaboration with local biz Superproductuers.

CopperBay has proven so popular with the French crowd that they've opened a second very successful outpost in Marseille as well as, more recently, taken up residence as the hotel bar in the swanky Paris Lancaster.

ROQUETTINI

Not only is a grind or two of fresh pepper a great garnish, but the Roquettini—*roquette* is the French word for arugula—is a wonderful example of the fresh, vegetal Mediterranean approach that CopperBay brings to cocktails.

3 cherry tomatoes

Handful of arugula

1⅔ oz. vodka

1 tbsp. fresh lemon juice

1½. tsp. white balsamic vinegar

1 dash simple syrup

3 dashes garlic bitters

1. Add the tomatoes and arugula to a cocktail shaker and muddle.

2. Add the remaining ingredients to the cocktail shaker with ice, shake well for 10 to 15 seconds, and double strain into a chilled cocktail glass.

3. Garnish with freshly ground pepper and, if desired, a pickled shallot.

LE SYNDICAT

51 Rue du Faubourg Saint-Denis, 75010 Paris

Le Syndicat's claim to fame is a 100 percent made in France approach using only domestic ingredients like Cognac, Armagnac, Calvados, and local liqueurs.

Luxury French products like Cognac have an impressive global reputation but are often overlooked in France, especially by the younger generation. Le Syndicat actively reminds the newest crop of barhoppers that these spirits are seriously good. Rather than a pedantic or in-your-face approach, they keep it fun and light-hearted like their tagline: "Where grandpa's spirits go gangsta."

They don't just convince with quality cocktails, but also with an effortlessly cool vibe that connects to a youthful and trendy client base. The bar is not far from the Gare du Nord in an area where Asian fruit and veg stands alternate with African barbers, and tasty traditional curries are served next door to hip, new bistros. Here neighborhood locals rub elbows with Parisians who cross town expressly for cocktails made with *la touche française*. There is something just right about a bar that celebrates all things French being located in this pocket that is a perfect example of the modern-day melting pot of Paris.

Once you find the hidden-in-plain-sight entrance amongst the walls of graffiti and promotional posters, the edgy assuredness continues inside. Exposed sheet-rock walls and visible soundproofing give it a rawness that feels like you've been admitted entry to your idolized older sibling's basement bedroom where all the really cool stuff goes down.

And while all the decor and design may seem nonchalant, a lot of thought that has gone into it all. The predominantly hip-hop soundtrack is a tip of the hat to

all the artists who have been influential in increasing the visibility of spirits like Cognac. The current menu celebrates the domestic, not just with local ingredients but collaborations with well-known French chefs to determine just the right culinary approach to take with the cocktails. And deceptively simple drinks are created on a solid foundation of technique and knowledge.

But you don't even need to know all of that to simply sit back and sip something very French in le Syndicat.

APOLLINAIRE

This easy cocktail is a perfect example of the many different ways that le Syndicat can combine French ingredients for a delicious cocktail.

1 oz. Loire Valley Sauvignon Blanc

½ oz. raspberry eau de vie

1⅓ oz. fresh grapefruit juice

⅚ oz. simple syrup

½ egg white or ½ tbsp. aquafaba

1. Put all of the ingredients in a blender with 3 big ice cubes and blend.
2. Strain the drink into a chilled rocks glass over ice.
3. Garnish with grapefruit zest on top of the foam.

ABRICOT

189 Rue Saint-Maur, 75010 Paris

An expat duo recently opened Abricot, featuring cocktails and plant-based dishes that showcase the owners' American, Ashkenazi, and Mexican/Southwestern backgrounds.

Though not long on the scene, Abricot has quickly made a splash with the city's expat crowd and features frequently on their social media feeds. Allison Kave and Jennifer Crain took over what was formerly a standard corner bar, the kind you find all over France. With a lot of elbow grease, they very intentionally created an all-inclusive atmosphere where everyone feels welcome. On arrival, incoming guests even get a tiny welcome drink served in a vintage glass. And while all are welcome, Abricot was also conceived to be a space where solo women specifically feel comfortable enjoying a drink at the bar without feeling awkwardly alone.

The drink menu includes a tight collection of house creations that tweak classic templates. There is currently one option for red, white, and sparkling wine as well as local beer and cider. The food menu features fun snacks like lime salt popcorn, a taco trio, and halvah chocolate chip cookies.

As part of a younger generation of bars in Paris, you'll find a lot of things that appeal to a certain demographic of drinkers like vegetarian snacks and eco-friendly practices. Abricot also strives to be part of a bigger community—the bar got off the ground with crowdfunding. It's the kind of place that closes at midnight midweek, but might stay open a little later if people are having a great time.

With their focus on community, quality products, and food offerings that are less common in Paris, it's a nice package. It's also the kind of place that feels like more than just a bottom line for the owners, but a way to share and celebrate a lifestyle.

BARANAAN

7 Rue du Faubourg Saint-Martin, 75010 Paris

Baranaan is a speakeasy hidden behind a small café selling chai and snacks.

In 1949, the Bombay Prohibition Act was put in place in the Indian state of Maharashtra, imposing severe penalties for the consumption or possession of alcohol. The owners of Baranaan sought inspiration from this period for their speakeasy. They imagined thirsty residents of dry states taking nightly train rides to nearby states where it was still possible to consume spirits and cocktails. Thus, this Indian Prohibition Train of 1949 was born.

To hop on board, head into the bright storefront café and ask the staff to take you to the train. They lead you down an incense-perfumed hallway into the back room. The speakeasy is designed to resemble a train, complete with moving scenery outside its faux windows. Settle into a car and peruse the cocktail menu that runs with the theme, resembling little blue Indian passports.

Some of the cocktails use Indian spirits, like their G&T made with an Indian gin. Many of them incorporate ingredients popular in Indian cuisine, like timut pepper, cumin, and coconut. They offer a selection of Indian whiskies and the bar's own branded artisanal beer. The street snacks are Franco-Indian fusion with the meat skewers and various naan options being popular choices.

The overall result is a romanticized, colorful, more polished version of a train ride in Prohibition India. With its location in Saint-Denis it's somewhat camouflaged in plain sight amongst other Indian restaurants on the streets of this multicultural neighborhood. Its hidden nature deters passersby. The need to commit to a technicolor Bollywood take on history keeps out the old folks. And, sure, the tiny whiff of cultural appropriation gives pause to some anglophones. But that just helps keep the tourists out.

This bar's demographic is young Parisians stopping in to celebrate birthdays or surprise their dates in a place that makes for cool Instagram stories. And aren't speakeasies all just romantic versions of a different reality? So, stop in here to party with the young and carefree crowd.

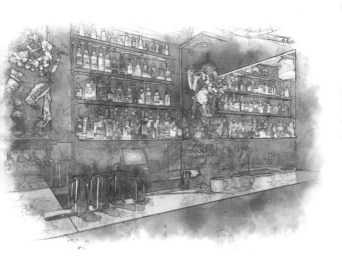

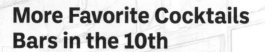

More Favorite Cocktails Bars in the 10th

GRAVITY
44 Rue des Vinaigriers, 75010 Paris

LE RENARD
38 Rue de Sambre-et-Meuse, 75010 Paris

LAVOMATIC
30 Rue René Boulanger, 75010 Paris

BONHOMIE
22 Rue d'Enghien, 75010 Paris

DIVINE
61 Rue d'Hauteville, 75010 Paris

For Local Terrace Café Life

CHEZ PRUNE
36 Rue Beaurepaire, 75010 Paris

LE FLORÉAL
73 Rue du Faubourg du Temple, 75010 Paris

LE MAURI 7
46 Rue du Faubourg Saint-Denis, 75010 Paris

11th, 12th & 13th Arrondissements
Oberkampf / Bastille / Quai de Bercy

The 11th, like its nearby neighbor, the 10th, has a frenetic and lively energy and is basically bursting with busy bars. And while the 12th and 13th are a little more laid-back, you can find a few bars with the same level of energy if you know where to look.

17th

16th

7t

15th

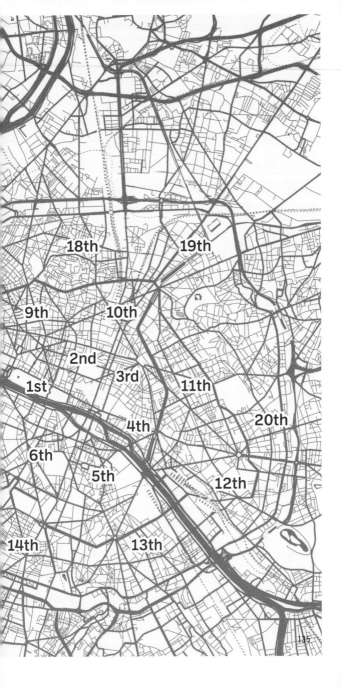

18th

19th

9th

10th

2nd

3rd

1st

11th

4th

20th

6th

5th

12th

14th

13th

135

MONSIEUR ANTOINE

17 Ave Parmentier, 75011 Paris

Monsieur Antoine is an unassuming cocktail bar that sticks to an MO of making quality cocktails in a no-fuss, friendly atmosphere defined by low-key conviviality that feels much more authentic than some of the flash and faff of fancier cocktail bars. This is a quality lacking in many of the more student-type party bars with cheap beers, overly sweet cocktails, and shots that populate this same street.

Monsieur Antoine's interior is a simple setup with tall stools around the bar and chairs around sturdy old trunks that serve as tables. It's minimalist chic. And the same could be said of the cocktail presentation. Their house creations are presented with a stylish simplicity. They come in delicate colors and might be garnished with a small fresh flower or served "up on the rocks" in a tall coupe over a large jagged block of ice.

The cocktails themselves offer a little something for everyone, but nearly all have just a touch of something less familiar, more exotic. For example, a seemingly easy-going vodka cocktail with kiwi honey syrup is elevated by the addition of Penja pepper. They reach beyond the basics with ingredients like grilled almond syrup or Jamaican pepper syrup, made in-house. They've even been known to occasionally rim a cocktail with caterpillar salt. These bartenders clearly enjoy creating cocktails, which translates into good drinks and an enthusiasm for sharing them with clients. They also serve artisanal beers and natural wine alongside a menu of quality bar snacks like hummus and jamon.

This hidden gem is where the neighborhood's relaxed crowd goes to chill out with friends while listening to the alternative rock favored by the owners. Occasionally DJs come in to play sets. Otherwise, it's just good food, good drinks, and good times for locals with good taste, but without a lot of pretense about it.

MOONSHINER

5 Rue Sedaine, 75011 Paris

This speakeasy, hidden behind a meat locker door in a Paris pizzeria, plays heavily on the American Prohibition theme. Just walk straight to the back of Pizza da Vito and push open the unmarked metal door to travel a century back in time. While Prohibition-style speakeasies are no longer a novelty, this one is a beauty in terms of style. Many give a few winks and nods to the Noble Experiment, but here the brick walls, metal ceiling tiles, art deco details, vintage gramophone, and chesterfield sofas all set the scene for an illicit evening of drinking bathtub gin.

Fortunately, here, you will be drinking something superior to moonshine. The staff are well-versed and also welcome guest bartenders from some of Europe's top cocktail bars. That means, in addition to a local crowd, there's also a big international contingent. The cocktail list includes house creations mixed with a variety of base spirits and their Barrel-Aged Vieux Carré is a popular choice. For something more modern-day mobster, they have about a hundred whiskeys on offer. They happily make classics, so a dry gin martini is also a theme-appropriate choice. I've even been served a cocktail in a flask hidden in a cutout old book.

As smoking becomes more and more prohibited these days, somehow it seems sort of fitting that they have a *fumoir* on the premises. And, the bonus of having the pizzeria in front is being able to easily soak up those strong drinks afterward with a slice.

It's a low-lit intimate place that would be perfect for hushed conversations or flirty dates. But this part of Paris is thick with bars and, as a result, many, many barhoppers have discovered this blind pig hidden in a pizza joint. As they don't take reservations, the place is bustling most nights with both locals and visitors. But, really, that might make it even more like a real, rowdy, roaring 1920s hidden bar.

FRÉQUENCE

20 Rue Keller, 75011 Paris

Fréquence attracts local lovers of both music and mixology, as it successfully combines these two personal passions of co-owners Matthieu Biron and Guillaume Quenza.

The bar decor is no-frills but stylish, with distressed wooden floors and large floor-to-ceiling windows. Tall stools and tables are scattered around the small space, but it's best to sit at the bar where you have a front row view of the turntable and the hundreds of LPs that line the back wall. The soundtrack leans toward groovy Motown, soul, funk, and reggae.

The bar menu features a handful of well-executed house cocktails as well as a refreshing section devoted to highballs, including a classic made with whisky and a more offbeat umeshu version. These highballs hint at the Japanese influences found in the menu, which also includes saké and Asahi beer by the can. The staff is skilled enough to pull off classic cocktail requests. And the whisky offerings are healthy; Quenza came from one of the city's better known whisky bars, Sherry Butt. They are right on trend in terms of bubbly drinks with both pet nat and French cider.

Nicely priced small plates made with fresh and seasonal ingredients like asparagus with ricotta cheese, ceviche, chicken skewers, and dumplings go beyond your basic bar nosh and into elevated snack territory.

The space is small, so arrive early to get a seat at the bar. And be prepared for crowds on weekends when they bring in DJs and stay open until 4 a.m.

HOUSE GARDEN

8 Rue Richard Lenoir, 75011 Paris

While there is a lot of talk about low-proof cocktails, only House Garden takes this trend all the way with a full menu of lower alcohol mixed drinks.

Prior to co-founding House Garden, Olivier Martinez worked in Dubai where he mastered no- and low-alcohol cocktails. He and business partner Yann Salentin have put this know-how to work at House Garden, creating options that allow customers the possibility of just one more drink without the morning-after repercussions.

They still mix with all of the usual spirits, but at dialed-down levels. For example, a classic might come as a reverse version, so a Manhattan would be two parts vermouth to one part whisky instead of the reverse. But this duo goes beyond just turning classics on their heads and digs in when it comes to developing new cocktail menus. They also run the potential drinks through a few lucky taste testers to input on any final tweaks prior to publishing the final menu.

What results are low-alcohol cocktails that are not lightweights in terms of flavor, including pleasant surprises like garlic or mushroom. They also incorporate advanced techniques like spherification for liquid orbs to serve alongside cocktails or dehydration for ham as a garnish.

Olivier and Yann want guests to feel at home in their "house" and the set-up invites conviviality. Different seating configurations make it easy to either chat in larger groups at the taller table or settle into small groups on the booth along the wall. A few stools at the bar provide a front row view of the shaking and stirring. Windows run the street-front side and, weather permitting, are open to let in lots of light, air, and life from the

lively neighborhood. Small plate options like guacamole and charcuterie encourage sharing to further facilitate the friendly vibe.

House Garden is the kind of bar that is just under the radar enough to not pull in a huge international crowd (yet), but still cool enough to pull in some really interesting locals.

ELIXIR DES DRUIDES

The team at House Garden creates simple cocktails with complex flavors by carefully selecting unusual ingredients like chouchen, a fermented beverage from Brittany that can be replaced with mead in the recipe if you can't find the real thing.

1⅓ oz. Cilantro-Infused Sweet Vermouth

⅔ oz. chouchen

⅔ oz. elderflower liqueur

1 tsp. fresh lemon juice

1. Combine all of the ingredients in a mixing glass filled with ice, stir until well chilled, and strain into a chilled rocks glass or goblet over ice.

Cilantro-Infused Sweet Vermouth: Combine 2 cups fresh cilantro with 1 bottle of sweet vermouth and let infuse for 90 minutes. Strain into a clean bottle and refrigerate to store.

RED HOUSE

1bis Rue de la Forge Royale, 75011 Paris

This lively little dive bar packs in a fun crowd, from neighborhood residents to locals who trek across town for the relaxed, convivial vibe. I've even seen a few famous actresses, both French and American, letting their hair down here. While there are plenty of bars in the busy Bastille area, this is one that delivers something more unique. Longhorns hang behind the bar and a Metallica pinball machine pings in the corner. The American flag pinned to the ceiling is a nod to the origins of owner, Joe Boley, who brings a lot of his own personality to this place.

Regulars order from a nicely priced and seasonally changing cocktail menu painted on the mirror behind the bar. Their spicy, chili-infused tequila Wild West Side has kicked off many a great night of dancing and fun beneath the slowly twisting giant disco ball. There's also beer on tap and their famous 5 euro Negroni ("Because they love you"). No one is going to judge you for downing a shot or a simple rum and Coke. You can also feel comfortable going with a stiff martini and knowing it will be made well. But, in true divey style, what you won't really find here is wine (although you may get the occasional bottle of Prosecco).

Energy here is high and it's definitely a spot for those who seek fun over fancy. DJs regularly set up in the tiny front corner to amp up the ambiance with rock music. Boley and partner, Jen Riley, have created a real community in a place where it takes only a visit or two for the bartender to know your name. The cool mom-and-pop catering operation Emperor Norton brings the pub grub to another level with tacos, wings, nachos, and other Cali-inspired snacks. Red House also organizes seasonal events like Super Bowl viewings on their big screen, an annual Thanksgiving potluck, and a 4th of July crawfish boil that draws not only homesick expats but locals looking to dive into a bit of Americana.

GANG OF FOUR

Who doesn't love an equal parts cocktail? This recipe by Red House owner, Joseph Boley, is a surprising mix of ingredients that work wonderfully.together and might just be the makings of the next modern classic.

⅔ oz. Vida Mezcal

⅔ oz. Benedictine

⅔ oz. St. Germaine

⅔ oz. fresh lime juice

1. Combine all of the ingredients in a cocktail shaker with ice, shake well for 10 to 15 seconds, and strain into a chilled cocktail glass.

LE CALBAR

82 Rue de Charenton, 75012 Paris

*C*aleçon is the French word for boxers (as in the under-pants kind). When combined with the word "bar" you get the name of this cheeky little neighborhood spot tucked away on an otherwise quiet street. Here, amiable bartenders stir and shake cocktails in button-up shirts, bow ties, and nothing but boxers below the bar. Don't be misled into thinking this is seedy; rather, it's pure playfulness and innocent fun. In fact, you may not even notice the lack of trousers until someone steps out from behind the bar.

This unusual idea came to owners, Christophe Sichanh and Thierry Malikian, over a few drinks in their off-hours from a high-end hotel bar job. They wanted to create a venue that served the same quality of drinks but with a more whimsical ambiance. While suspenders, bow ties, and classic cocktails played on the very prominent Prohibition vibe of the time, they definitely set themselves apart with their "bottomless" concept.

Inside, Le Calbar gives off industrial curio parlor vibes. Youthful locals and the cocktail curious hang around the high table in the front area sharing tasty bar snacks or lounge along the chesterfield sofa that runs the length of the back wall. The shareable food menu includes items like guacamole and cheese plates plus tasty snacks in jars from eco-friendly, locally-focused Super Producteur.

The team continues to evolve to ensure clients always feel welcome. The menu includes drinks with on-trend cocktail ingredients like mezcal but also options for those looking for something more accessible like vodka or elderflower. Technique is on point and classics are done with care. Their creations can be inspired by classics like the Don't Be Chai, a Manhattan twist made with chai-infused rum, or something all their own. The Surprize Me is a popular choice for those who like to leave the decision to the pros.

Not surprisingly, the crowd is young and enthusiastic. Le Calbar has even been known to suggest nights where guests are invited to join in by sipping cocktails in their own boxer shorts. And the concept has been successful enough that they've opened a second outpost in Switzerland.

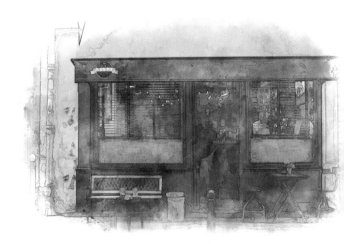

LE 18 OBERKAMPF

18 Rue Oberkampf, 75011 Paris

Jazz-loving locals reserve space at this cheerful wine bar for the weekly Wednesday jam sessions.

Owned by American Josh Goldstein and Lebanese Toni Fares, Le 18 Oberkampf is a wonderfully welcoming venue for people to both enjoy wine and engage with multicultural artistic and culinary programming. Every month a new artist in residence is celebrated at Le 18 with a display of their work that is kicked off by a opening, with wine, of course. For a more pedagogical approach, they also offer tasting workshops of wine paired with small dishes.

But beneath all this fun is a foundation of solid wine, which their Scottish cavist Craig Stevenson delights in helping patrons discover. In addition to the wine, Stevenson pours a mean G&T and has created drinks for the bar, like Auld One.

Like any self-respecting wine bar they serve up delicious plates of cheese and charcuterie, best eaten at the window table in front. From this vantage you can watch both locals bumping elbows at the bar and the Parisian life passing by the window. All of this is packaged in a venue with a modern and cheery decor, inspired by one of the owner's grandmothers.

It's the kind of place that engenders smiles—and for more than just the wine.

AULD ONE

This recipe by Craig Stevenson and Jules Bernard for the third birthday of Le 18 incorporates wine from Château le Devoy Martine, a house the bar has been collaborating with since 2020 for their own branded selection. As Stevenson explains, the drink's name "references the Auld Alliance, the ancient political, social, and cultural tie between France and Scotland; in this instance embracing the fusion of rich wine from the south of France and smoky whisky."

⅔ oz. Rozelieures Single Malt Whisky

1 oz. red wine (recipe calls for Selection le 18 Carignan Mourvèdre from Château le Devoy Martine, IGP Terres du Midi)

2 tsp. verjus

1 tsp. orange liqueur

1 dash cocoa bitters

½ tsp. simple syrup

1. Combine all of the ingredients in a mixing glass with ice, stir to chill, and strain into a large wineglass over ice.

2. Garnish with a slice of blood orange.

LA BUVETTE

67 Rue Saint-Maur, 75011 Paris

Cool kids with bedhead hair park their Vespas and sardine into a tiny wine bar in the hip 11th arrondissement. Welcome to Buvette, where the initiated arrive early and order cult natural wines by the bottle to drink on site (count on paying less if you take it to go).

Owner Camille Fourmont's criteria for choosing wines is simple: it's what she likes. Selection is limited but strong with nicely priced options from natural wine hotbeds like Beajoulais and the Loire Valley, plus a handful of harder to source, sought-after bottles.

La Buvette is a *cave à manger* so ordering a small plate of food with your wine is obligatory. Fourmont worked at Chateaubriand and Le Dauphin, both of which have plenty of caché and clout on the Parisian food scene with their acclaimed farm-to-table dishes, long lines, and hard to get reservations. She's clearly gained insight into creating tasty plates and serves small dishes that pair nicely with her wine.

So far, so good. But, it's also worth knowing that the clientele—and sometimes staff—can be a bit insider and territorial about this hidden gem they discovered over a decade ago. With the small real estate and early closing time (10 p.m.) it's rare to find the place when it isn't packed with wine enthusiasts working through the trendy tipples and talking about them in Franglais.

This is definitely not a good place to go if you are in a large group.

It's not just the tasty bites and curated wine list that appeals, but the well-designed space itself. Clean white square tiles contrast nicely against funky old floor tiles and artfully distressed portions of wall. Bottles line sturdy wooden shelves and a minimalist feel emphasizes the chic in its shabby-chic appeal.

A few years back Fourmont co-authored *La Buvette: Recipes and Wine Notes from Paris*. The book and several write-ups in the international press were a siren call to visiting foodies and wine buffs, meaning the previously rather local crowd is somewhat now more diluted with well-intentioned tourists. So, while this popular little wine bar may be a victim of its own success, it's worth a stop for hardcore oenophiles to find out what all the fuss is about at this pocket-sized natural wine institution.

SEPTIME LA CAVE

3 Rue Basfroi, 75011 Paris

The French excel at enjoying everyday life, whether it's the simple act of making a family meal or an easy aperitif amongst friends. Septime la Cave is a good example of this.

Neighborhood residents stop into this tiny shop to pick up a bottle of some lesser-known small producer wine for a weekday dinner, but they usually linger just a little longer as it's also a bar. They'll likely indulge in a glass of trendy natural wine with a small plate of anchovies or thick slices of homemade terrine served with crusty bread. Just another day in the life of the unselfconsciously hip Parisian.

While many tourists are likely to vie for reservations at its Michelin-starred big sister restaurant, Septime, the true Parisian makes this spot a part of their weekly routine. Unlike Septime the restaurant, there are no reservations here, so be prepared to get there early enough to score one of the few stools at the counter, balance your bottle on wine cartons, or spill out onto the sidewalk with other festive guests.

A chalkboard menu lists the small selection of regularly rotating bar snacks and staff are happy to provide suggestions. This is especially helpful as the place specializes in small and natural winemakers, so it's useful to have a little guidance. La Cave pulls in plenty of cool kids from the food and drink industry, so you're likely to rub elbows with locals who know their way around the city's restaurants and bars. And fortunately, it's also just across the way from the other no-reservations establishment in the Septime family, Clamato, making it an ideal pre-dinner stop before heading to its tasty sister venue for fresh oysters and sustainably sourced fish.

Basically, if you want a quiet glass of Côtes du Rhône with guaranteed seating, head for your nearest corner café. But if you want to experience the life of the young on-trend Parisian, go here. If you can't deal with the standing room only, make like the locals and just grab a bottle to go.

LE BARON ROUGE

1 Rue Théophile Roussel, 75012 Paris

Any mention of Le Baron Rouge is sure to elicit contented sighs and complimentary murmurs from the city's locals. Although this little wine bar regularly appears on lists of hidden gems and "under the radar" recommendations, the off-the-beaten location in the 12th arrondissement means less tourists and more Parisians.

While at first glance it may look like any other Paris café with a standard red awning and bottles lining the large shop front windows, this unpretentiously authentic bar is so much more as it envelops thirsty guests in the noisy bustle of neighborhood life. Le Baron Rouge is just off the large and lively Marché d'Aligre, which is open six days a week and pulls in Parisians from all over the city for their weekly shop. Once the shopping baskets are bursting with fresh veg, fruits, flowers, and meats, these same Parisians treat themselves to a well-earned drink and a snack at the bar. Later in the day, the residents of the quartier congregate here for an apéro.

Chalkboards hang behind the counter listing the many wines on offer and clients buy by the glass or carafe for just a few bucks from the many barrels stacked up against the wall. Simple charcuterie and cheese plates complete the offering. On Sundays, patrons enjoy fresh oysters to wash down with crisp whites—only in oyster season, of course!

The scene is jocularly jostling and service is frenetic, fun, and friendly rather than fussy. But this early evening and weekend chaos is part of the charm. It's rare to find available seating inside, so everyone spills out onto the sidewalk, balancing numerous bottles on barrels, strollers, nearby cars, or whatever makeshift tables can be found.

Like any truly self-respecting French venue, staff take an afternoon break and the bar closes for lunch, Sunday evenings, and all-day Monday, so do check hours before making the trip. For an even more local experience, come equipped with an empty bottle to fill for takeaway and enjoy it with dinner in your room or with a picnic of goodies from the Marché d'Aligre.

MARTIN

24 Bd du Temple, 75011 Paris

Confidently cool foodies and oenophiles frequent this rough-hewn wine bar for exceptional seasonal small plates paired with bottles from a playful list.

When former Au Passage bartender Löic Martin co-founded this diamond in the rough, he chose an old PMU as the location. These are ubiquitous betting parlors where hopeful Parisians pick lottery numbers and buy scratch tickets. But they generally sell cigarettes and include a small bar. Typically utilitarian and not fancy, they are an integral part of French daily life. Much remains of the former incarnation of this establishment with an exposed stone wall and a worn wooden bar, giving off a rough insouciance that is a big part of its appeal. Here, no one will stress about spilling a few drops of natural wine on the tabletops while clinking glasses with the other cool kids.

Löic Martin is a naturally friendly host and converses animatedly in English or French with regulars on the glassed-in veranda. This all-welcoming approach extends to the drinks menu. A few artisanal local beers stand alongside more cheap and cheerful industrial bottled options. Plenty of G&Ts provide occasion to try a variety of more unusual gins. There are a few options of wine by the glass and a much larger number of bottles—and this is the place to enjoy a bottle with friends. It's best to ask for guidance from the knowledgeable staff to discover some of the hidden gems or unusual varietals.

Martin gets packed so go late afternoon before the kitchen opens. Enjoy a glass as you share table space with the team getting in a staff meal before starting food service. From 7 p.m. onward, small plates from the chalkboard menu are available and well worth staying for.

When the terrace is full but the weather is nice, a few ad hoc barrel tables appear outside for those waiting for seating inside.

CAFÉ CHARBON

109 Rue Oberkampf, 75011 Paris

Founded in 1863, this airy, atypical, antique-chic brasserie is one of the oldest spots for a drink on the busy Rue Oberkampf.

Café Charbon has wowed guests with its grand decor for over a century. Huge mirrors adorn the walls of the high-ceilinged room that still bare beautiful old painted murals. Vintage floor tiles, original fixtures, and the metal bar, complete with uneven areas from years of use, give that palpable sense of Paris's past. Somewhat newer are the multiple fringed lampshades in rose, blush, and amber tones that dangle dramatically from the ceiling. A mezzanine allows you to get an eye on all of this from above as well.

Richard Debray added a fresh enthusiasm since taking over a decade or so ago. He's been an ambitious chef and run other Paris restaurants, but his dream had always been to own Café Charbon. While the kitchen here has served standard French fare since its opening, Debray modernized the dishes with Asian influences and a made-in-house approach to ingredients (not as common as you might think in France).

The cocktail menu features crowd pleasers like the Moscow Mule and modern classics like the Penicillin and Porn Star Martini. A selection of beer is available in bottles or on tap. With a list conceived to succeed in a restaurant, a glass of wine is a great choice here. Heck, make it a bottle, because this is the kind of place locals linger for an afternoon and suddenly realize it's time to stay for dinner or dance to DJs. And the real party people continue through to the wee hours of the morning with more drinks and dancing at their attached concert and events space, Nouvelle Casino.

Café Charbon is no stranger to the pages of guidebooks, so it naturally pulls in plenty of tourists. But it's also still a favorite haunt of the neighborhood residents. Speaking to a friend who lived down the street, she tells me she has been a loyal client for 25 years. Even after her recent move, she still crosses town for it.

LA FINE MOUSSE

4 bis Av. Jean Aicard, 75011 Paris

La Fine Mousse was one of the city's first craft beer bars, helping to shift the needle of French appreciation for artisanal brewing.

While France has had a significant history of independent brewing, that tradition was lost over the ages and had a hard time gaining a new foothold in a country full of wine lovers. Fortunately, a trio of Frenchmen—Romain Thieffry, Cyril Lalloum, and Laurent Cicurel—developed a taste for artisanal brews and teamed up with the owner of a local beer shop, Simon Thillou, to create a venue dedicated to celebrating this craft. Thus, in 2012, La Fine Mousse was born, providing interesting alternatives to the ubiquitous industrial Heineken and 1664 found in bars all over town.

This team did more than build a space that they personally found lacking in the city, but helped to break down stereotypes about beer and educate the Parisian public. La Fine Mousse has long been organizing events around beer and offering workshops. Fast forward a decade and the capital now has a thriving craft beer scene and an annual beer festival.

While there are currently many more places to enjoy beer of this variety now, loyal locals still return to this frontrunner to taste something from their 20 regularly changing kegs, or pick up one of 150 or so different bottled options. Not long after opening, they added a restaurant across the way where beer lovers can enjoy a dinner pairing with their favorite beverage.

When La Fine Mousse opened, the explosion of French artisanal breweries hadn't happened yet so they began—and continue—with an international offering. However, they've subsequently opened a second outpost, La Mousse & La Robe, which features exclusively domestic craft beer and spirits.

An interesting group of locals hangs out here. It helps that, though the bar is near the busy Oberkampf area, it's set off on a quiet street and so is missed by the throngs of bar crawlers and rather is a determined destination for serious beer lovers.

BATEAU EL ALAMEIN

10 Port de la Gare, 75013 Paris

Bateau el Alamein is a quirky purple *péniche* with a terrace garden café and a below deck concert venue.

The banks of the Seine are punctuated by *péniches* of all shapes, sizes, and states of repair. These large barges have played an important role in Paris's history and economy, transporting goods along the river. During World War II some were put into service as floating hospitals. Nowadays some transport tourists across the city for views of its famous attractions. However, many simply sit stationary on the river and serve primarily as private houseboats, bars, and clubs. While most of those located in central Paris and high-traffic areas get a lot of tourists, locals have their personal favorites, which are often on less frequented stretches of the Seine.

Bateau el Alamein, moored a bit out from the center, is a regular favorite of locals who like their boat a little fun and a little funky. This happy-go-lucky *péniche* opens in summer months to welcome guests onto the plant-covered terrace where they enjoy so-so cocktails and cheap beer on the brightly colored folding metal tables and chairs. Sure, it feels a little janky, but that's part of the charm. And once you are settled in, watching the sun set over the city, feeling the slight movement of the water, even a mediocre drink goes down great. Below deck, big disco balls reflect light over the bright blue walls of the concert hall where musicians entertain with jazz sets, old French *chansons*, and more.

There are a handful of other *péniches* and plenty of open-air cafés and bars on this length of the river, so it's easy to make Bateau el Alamein a starting or ending point for a waterfront bar hop.

More Fun Spots in the Area

FIFTY FIFTY
74 Rue Jean-Pierre Timbaud, 75011 Paris

CAFÉ MODERNE
19 Rue Keller, 75011 Paris

BLUEBIRD
12 Rue Saint-Bernard, 75011 Paris

CHAMBRE NOIRE
4 Bd Jules Ferry, 75011 Paris

FULGURANCES
5 Rue Alexandre Dumas, 75011 Paris

Cocktail lovers should also head to Fifty Fifty, Café Moderne, and Bluebird, while wine drinkers will appreciate Chambre Noire and Fulgurances.

15th & 16th Arrondissements
**Vaugirard / Beaugrenelle /
Bois de Boulogne**

With a rather staid and well-heeled population, things can get slightly stuffy around here. But don't let the occasional airs and graces deter you, because if you know where to look, you can find some classy but cool spots for a drink.

17th

16th

7t

15th

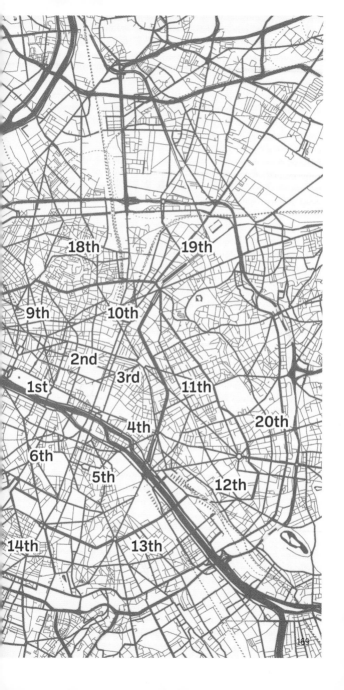

LE PERCHOIR PORTE DE VERSAILLES

2 Av de la Prte de la Plaine, 75015 Paris

While the farm-to-fork policies of this rooftop bar and restaurant are commendable, Left Bank locals really come here for the panoramic views of the city.

Trendy Parisians are all too familiar with Le Perchoir Group and its chain of uber-designed bars and restaurants perched upon the city's rooftops—the name even means "the perch." The opening of this particular outpost thrilled residents of *la rive gauche* as the first of the group to arrive on this side of the river. But even bigger headline-grabbing news was that it would be located next to the world's largest rooftop farm, from whom they source produce.

The interior design of all of their venues is strong, but this one is particularly ambitious. The architectural agency wanted to highlight the synergy with the neighboring farm, so nature is front and center. Le Perchoir is airy, green, and leafy and the bar is covered with handmade ceramic bamboo stalks. The designers worked in as many natural materials as possible. It gives off some serious vacation vibes and would be worth a visit even without the stunning city views. It's all very Instagram friendly.

The drinks selection is pretty standard. Wine and beer are good choices. Cocktails reflect basics that go down easily. While it's laudable that the restaurant program goes very short-circuit, the food can be hit or miss. Best to go for a drink, and potentially stay if it looks like a good day for their dishes.

Being located on the periphery of the city means shorter lines and less waiting, compared to their central, more hyped locations. This means it pulls in a crowd of thirty-somethings that is trendy—but not trendy enough to be bothered crossing the river. It's also situated on the sixth floor of a pavilion of one of the city's major conference centers, so it gets a smattering of professionals in the area for events.

ILVOLO BAR OF HOTEL NOVOTEL VAUGIRARD

257 Rue de Vaugirard, 75015 Paris

Located a little off the beaten path, Ilvolo is one of the city's best kept secrets for a low-key drink with a view of the Eiffel Tower.

With its iconic rooftops and relatively flat landscape allowing clear views of legendary landmarks, Paris is a delight to see from above. Now that's no secret as is evidenced by the fact that the city's rooftop real estate is consistently packed, making it a challenge to score a seat for a simple drink with a view. However, the Ilvolo Bar atop the Novotel Vaugirard hotel is indeed a little local secret. It's not just the nondescript exterior of the hotel, but the location in a primarily residential area that doesn't draw a lot of tourists that makes it much easier to grab a spot in this bar.

For years the bar was only open during summer months and had a hard time finding its footing. A recent hotel renovation resulted in an overdue facelift and creation of an indoor space where clients can settle into the contemporary colorful seating to contemplate the horizon in all seasons and weather. Metal latticework around the windows mirrors that of the Iron Lady, which is the star of the scenery show. But spend more time staring out at Paris for an occasional glimpse of the hot-air balloon slowly rising from and returning to the Parc André Citroën, a close-up view of the nearby apartment terraces of regular Parisian life, and more of the city's notable landmarks.

The revamp brought some welcome improvements to the food and drinks program as well. A nice selection of beer and wine is on offer plus bottled cocktails created by local mixologist Matthias Giroud. The drinks play with presentation and may come in a ceramic eggshell or capped by a fancy garnish.

The improvements in food and drink have been accompanied by a slight price hike, taking it above the norm in this neighborhood. But it's still well worth it for the views from this hidden gem.

TREIZE AU CLUBHOUSE: PARIS JEAN BOUIN

5 Av. de la Prte Molitor, 75016 Paris

Treize au Clubhouse gives the phrase "sports bar" a whole new meaning. This large and luminous restaurant and bar is located on the edge of the city just steps from the famous Rolland Garros tennis courts and the Jean Bouin stadium, which hosts the local rugby club and will be one of the venues used for the 2024 Olympics in Paris. It's right by the Bois de Boulogne, where active types take long runs, as well as a fitness center or two. This is an area known for athletics.

Its powerhouse pair of founders, Laurel Coker-Sanderson and Kaysa von Sydow, have managed to combine the charming southern hospitality of their other venue, Treize au Jardin, with the sporty sensibilities of the surroundings.

The interior is lovely, with mint-green chairs and wainscoting, a light parquet floor, and ceiling fans, making for a decor that feels like a cozy holiday home. A beauty of a bar takes up the full back wall. The sofa and relaxed chairs grouped around a distressed wooden table are perfect spots to settle in for a well-deserved drink after a walk around the nearby wooded area.

With a couple of screens to watch the matches, it's the chicest "sports bar" around. With its cool decor and healthy options menu, it's a refreshing detour from the beer, wings, and dozens-of-screens type of venue where you can typically catch a game.That means you can also get freshly squeezed juice in addition to wine, coffee, beer or something a little stronger. Here, as with their other venue, they celebrate organic, local, and sustainable ingredients.

When the weather warms up, they open the large terrace that overlooks the architecturally interesting stadium. And, it's also a kid-friendly spot, with children's menus and ice cream, making it a great destination for a drink with the family.

Being so out of the way, the only visitors Treize au Clubhouse draws are those coming for matches. But, on a typical day, it just pulls in a lot of locals from the surrounding residential neighborhood.

CRAVAN

17 Rue Jean de la Fontaine, 75016 Paris

Cravan is the perfect place to drink in your fantasy French life. Located in a historically registered building, this café has been renovated under new ownership but still retains all of its art nouveau appeal. Couple that with exceptional cocktails and you've got something special, made even better by the fact that it's far enough off the beaten path to avoid too many tourists who read about it in the latest high-profile list of the city's best bars.

Built by Hector Guimard—designer of some of Paris's most famous metro entrances—this location has been a bar and café since 1911. The belle époque beauty shines through on the inside with a well-worn zinc bar, fantastic murals, and vintage tiles and mirrors. Outside, classic French bistro chairs crowd the sidewalk terrace, welcoming Parisians for warm evening aperitifs and people watching.

What makes this café more than just a nostalgic nod to a charming era are the quality cocktails. With a drinks program created by Franck Audoux, author of *French Moderne: Cocktails from the Twenties and Thirties*, it's no surprise that the classics and house creations are worth a detour. The menu offers just enough to appeal to a full range of cocktail drinkers. Many are lower in alcohol and come in small delicate coupes, meaning you can easily appreciate a few for cocktail hour. Or stretch it out to a mini-dinner visit, ordering a few of their delicious small plates.

Cravan is out of the way, but it's still too good to have gone undiscovered and has been written up by international journalists with their fingers on the pulse of the Parisian drinks scene. Fortunately, it's still remote enough that the English you'll hear on the terrace is usually from the well-heeled international clientele living in this polished little pocket of Paris rather than those coming from afar.

Even the name feels romantic, taken from Arthur Cravan, Swiss poet, artist, boxer, and nephew of Oscar Wilde. It's heartening to see Paris venues seeking inspiration from the past while still creating something fresh and up to date.

LE BELAIR

116 Av. du Président Kennedy, 75016 Paris

In the rather staid arrondissement of the 16th, one unique building really stands out: La Maison de la Radio. This enormous circular complex, designed by architect Henry Bernard in 1963, houses the central services for Radio France, recording studios for many of its shows, a museum of broadcasting, a restaurant, and Le Belair.

Situated on the second floor of this structure, with views overlooking the Seine, Le Belair has a sleek design that radiates 1970s chic. Camel leather armchairs built with slightly futuristic curves, plush banquettes, and a dance floor that lights up all look back to that sexy decade. Rose gold mirrored slats cover the ceiling and reflect warm, flattering light onto the dancers.

This scene overlooks the Beaugrenelle skyline across the river with its tiny fleet of skyscraper hotels and apartment buildings. This somehow seems very fitting as the most noticeable of them is the crimson Novotel, built in 1976, also with elements of design that were very forward-thinking for the time. And if you score a window seat you can also get in a peek at the top of the Eiffel Tower.

Not many tourists come to this corner of the city and, if they do, would likely not guess they should just walk through the security checkpoint at the front entrance. Once on the ground floor, it still feels a little like a space in which you're not really supposed to be due to its after-business-hours emptiness. So, the crowd skews toward neighborhood residents and Radio France staff who clink colorful cocktails or slowly sip glasses of wine while decompressing from their daily grind.

While hours shift, currently the bar is only open Thursday through Saturday and occasionally midweek for scheduled concerts or events. DJs spin sets on Saturdays or special occasions. The restaurant, just a short flight of steps below, is also a highly designed space that is open most nights and serves French Asian fusion. Both tend to get busier much later in the evening.

LE DOKHAN'S HOTEL CHAMPAGNE BAR

117 Rue Lauriston, 75116 Paris

One of the city's oldest champagne bars is tucked away in an elegant nineteenth-century Haussmannian town house turned boutique hotel. While the impressive number of champagnes on offer is reason enough for sparkling wine lovers to cross town, Le Dokhan's beautiful bar itself is worth the trip. This historical neoclassical building is furnished with expertly selected antiques and custom-made pieces. Pale green walls, gold trim, and rich wooden flooring evoke a more elegant era. It's all about style and class at the city's ultimate bubbles bar. Works by Matisse and Picasso hang on the walls and the hotel elevator is kitted out in Louis Vuitton luggage leather and brass—riding it feels like being inside an LV trunk. It's also the kind of establishment where custom scents perfume the air.

In the mornings this stunning bar space is used as a super swanky breakfast room. But once the hotel's bacon and eggs crowd moves on, it's time for some serious cork popping. An afternoon clientele leisurely makes its way through for something sparkling on shopping and touring breaks. Once evening falls, candlelight casts an intimate glow over guests raising delicate champagne flutes of vintage fizz.

This is a good option for anyone from beginners to serious aficionados as the sommelier is always on hand to help navigate the 250 or so champagnes available. The collection covers small independent growers to large well-known brands. An extensive range also means that it's possible to find something at a comfortable price level.

In a hotel of this caliber, they know how to welcome guests, and extras include nice nibbles and weekly live jazz. And to really gild the lily, they offer an exceptional selection of caviar with suggestions for the perfect champagne pairing.

Of course, hotel guests can't resist a sip of something sparkling here. But you'll also get a good mix of champagne loving locals who regularly attend their tastings and educational events and in-the-know Parisians looking to impress a date with something special.

HOTEL SAINT JAMES

5 Pl. du Chancelier Adenauer, 75116 Paris

This chateau-hotel is an urban oasis secreted away in the 16th arrondissement with both a cozy library bar and verdant garden terrace.

It's impossible not to feel special in this neoclassic chateau that manages to combine the traditional and modern for a tastefully chic take on luxury. High-end interior designers who regularly feature on the pages of *Architectural Digest* layer in an eclectic mix of texture and material, playing graphic and natural elements against each other to a stylish end. Nearly everything— including the individual room numbers—is custom-made. It's the kind of place with an abundance of class and taste.

In addition, there's the location of Paris's first airfield, where hot-air balloons once touched down. This means a swath of green space remains in the city. So, not only is it set off somewhat remotely in the 16th, but the unusual abundance of undeveloped real estate has allowed for a walled-off garden around the premises. Intricate lawn furniture, greenhouses, and a pergola set the scene for a bucolic escape from the city fray over an al fresco aperitif in warm weather.

In winter months and on cooler nights, guests find a cozy hideaway in the romantic library bar with some 12,000 leather-bound volumes lining the walls, a spiral staircase, and a refined chic aesthetic. Laura Gonzalez, the latest designer to work her magic on this space, has retained the traditional British club feel of the bar with its wood panels and coffered ceiling but updated it with Iranian rugs and Indian cashmere.

Saint James is a private club as well as a hotel, meaning members can access many spaces around the clock. But the public is welcome in the bars and the restaurant in the evenings for a delicious taste of the luxe life. Or, to sneak in something during daytime hours, schedule an indulgent treatment at the spa and then enjoy a post-massage drink indoors or outdoors.

In short, this contemporary celebration of old Parisian style is where you go to mingle with chic city residents and club members over cocktails, mocktails, or an always-in-fashion glass of champagne.

DORIS BAR AT SIR WINSTON

5 Rue de Presbourg, 75016 Paris

The Sir Winston, off the Champs-Élysées, has the distinction of being named after U.K. prime minister Churchill as well as being one of the oldest pubs in Paris. Recently, its traditional club-like feel was updated with something lighter, brighter, and more modern. But like the P.M. after whom it's named, this British pub and brasserie has a naughty little secret. Beneath the sizable bar and restaurant is a more discrete speakeasy called Doris—named after English socialite Lady Doris Castlerosse with whom Churchill had an illicit affair.

And Doris is a looker! The bar is all decked out in polished wooden trim and panels, classic brass touches, soft velour booths, and dramatic carpet the color of crimson lipstick (maybe worn by Lady Castlerosse on her clandestine romantic rendezvous with Churchill?). Lamps are dim and candlelight reflects beautifully in the mottled mirrors that cover the walls, ceiling, and back of the bar. It's all very seductive.

But, much like a fanciful socialite, Doris can change on a whim. Quarterly, the bar collaborates with a new partner, be it an independent local liqueur brand or a cool cocktail lounge. The partner is given carte blanche to set the tone with their own ephemeral menu and concept that lasts only for a fleeting three months.

As a result, the drinks selection shifts depending on who's in bed with the bar and sometimes they can skew a little on the sweet side. But, given the indulgent surroundings, champagne is also an excellent option, and the decor is always worth the detour. A food menu is available with a selection of British and Indian bar snacks.

With its familiar pub atmosphere and being so close to the Arc de Triomphe, the Sir Winston is an easy draw for the city's tourists. But the recent revamp by trendy designer Laura Gonzales plus the ever-changing scene in the bar has renewed interest in this long-standing institution and it's tempting a cool and curious local crowd back in.

17th & 18th Arrondissements
Batignolles / Clichy / Montmartre

These two arrondissements are a melting pot of culture that juxtaposes the rough and charming. From the butte of Montmartre to the backstreets of Batignolles, there are pockets of tourist territory within a larger terrain of real local life with bars that pack in Parisians.

17th

16th

7t

15th

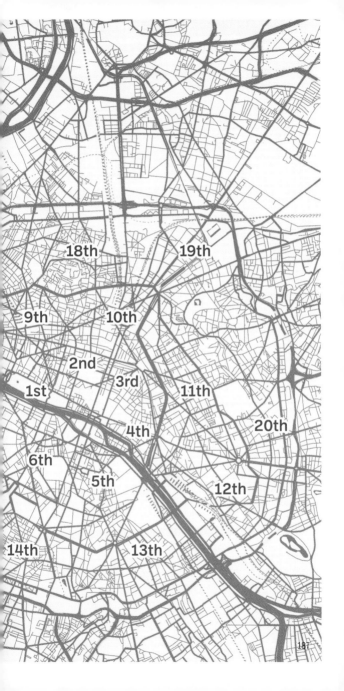

LE TRÈS PARTICULIER

Hôtel Particulier Montmartre,
23 Av. Junot Pavillon D, 75018 Paris

If you want to experience Le Très Particulier, you'll have to first find the hidden passageway behind the iron gateway off a quiet Montmartre backstreet that leads to this beautiful bar.

The hotel in which this little haven is hidden is a big part of its charm. What is now the stunning Hotel Particulier was a mansion built in the nineteenth century that housed some of the city's classiest residents—the Hermès family once called it home. It's now an exclusive hotel hideaway for fashionable visitors, many of the celebrity ilk. And while the hotel itself is certainly a destination mainly for tourists, the bar is a regular go-to for the city's chicest locals.

Le Très Particulier offers up three different spaces for sipping, each with their own appeal. The intimate and smoldering indoor bar is where the pretty people settle into crimson velvet armchairs against the dramatic fairytale-like backdrop of Garden of Eden wallpaper and sip creative cocktails by the glow of low lamps and candlelight. Just beyond is the glassed-in terrace with its bold black-and-white tile floors, armchairs, and abundance of lush plant life. Here you have a lovely view of the trees and gardens surrounding the hotel, which were designed by Louis Benech, also known for his work on Paris's famous Tuileries Gardens.

Finally, if you want to appreciate the ambience al fresco, there are plenty of iron tables and chairs outside in the garden so you can sip your cocktails beneath the trees.

While early evening can be calm, some nights see DJs, special celebrations like their fantastical Halloween galas, or cocktail events, which means it's packed and busy. This is a whimsical, rich, and truly bucolic escape from everyday life.

Le Très Particulier is open every day and never disappoints with its otherworldly charm that lets you slip peacefully into a surreal state of mind.

JUSTE UN DOIGT

The name of this cocktail translates to "just a finger," a reference to its bourbon base.

½ egg white or ½ tbsp. aquafaba

1⅔ oz. bourbon

2 turns of a pepper grinder

⅘ oz. fresh lemon juice

⅔ tsp. sugar

1. Add the egg white or aquafaba to a cocktail shaker and dry shake for 10 seconds.
2. Add the remaining ingredients to the shaker, fill halfway with ice, shake well for 10 to 15 seconds, and strain into a chilled cocktail glass.

TERASS HOTEL

12-14 Rue Joseph de Maistre, 75018 Paris

Tourists and locals alike take the elevator to the seventh floor of this Montmartre hotel for pretty drinks with an even prettier view. Founded in 1911, the Terass Hotel has passed from generation to generation of the same family for over a century. Having gone through various renovations and revamps, this landmark has arrived at a design sweet spot of contemporary chic that still recalls its beautiful bohemian past.

Topping it all off is a panoramic restaurant and rooftop bar, which is open and airy and definitely knows how to dress for the season. In spring and summer months the top is retracted, the windows open wide, and lush green and floral touches abound. In colder weather it gets all buttoned up, turns up the heat lamps, and puts on special winter events like a weekly raclette.

But it's the view that steals the show. Not only is the bar on the top floor of the hotel, but the hotel is at a higher elevation than most of the city. It's oriented in the right direction to catch Parisian rooftops, the Eiffel Tower, the nearby Montmartre cemetery, and the setting sun.

For drinks, they offer a small cocktail menu of house creations served in tiki mugs or with an abundance of garnish. Wine, beer, and bubbles are on offer, and the very nicely priced mulled cider is the best choice on cool nights.

No hotel guest will want to miss this, so there are usually just as many visitors as locals. Smart locals know it's best to head here at the opening hour of 3:30 p.m. when it's easy to snag a seat along the edge with an unobstructed view and while service is still personalized and unharried. Those who arrive later are there for the see-and-be-seen scene, and likely know someone who can help them sneak past the very long lines required to get in for a glimpse. Extra savvy locals know they can also reserve in the restaurant if they really want the guaranteed view late in the evening without the irritating wait.

L'HELICE

50 Rue d'Orsel, 75018 Paris

There was a time when Montmartre wasn't part of Paris but a village on the city's outskirts. Nowadays, even though its iconic cobblestone streets, charming steep staircases leading to the Sacré-Cœur, and legendary Moulin Rouge keep the butte teeming with tourists, there remains a strong sense of community and village mentality amongst its residents. Bars like L'Helice are where many of these locals like to congregate.

Here, you'll find a young and lively crowd around the beat-up barrels used as tables with cans of Red Bull or half-pints of beer. The table in the front window could be taken up by a couple of old friends meeting for an apéro, maybe with a dog in tow. This seating affords ample views of the street and the opportunity for pointed commentary on the people passing by. It also offers easy access to the bartender for quicker refills on the cheap and cheerful wine accompanied by a bit of friendly chitchat.

In a place like this it's not a fashionable interior design that draws in the locals. Rather, it's the lack of that kind of design. L'Helice is the same style of standard bar found in neighborhoods all over the capital with bright lighting, janky barstools, a basic metal counter, a few beers on tap, and a small selection of simple spirits. And this familiar environment clearly signals that it is not the latest concept bar. This is an authentic establishment where you know exactly what you are getting: a

straightforward French drinking experience. And what it lacks in trendy extras, it more than makes up for with a welcoming conviviality, which is really what's at the heart of any good drinking session.

If you get chummy with the bartender, he may even offer you a shot of bright green minty fresh Get 27 before you leave—and it would be rude not to take him up on it with a smile.

SUZE & TONIC

This is an easy and forgiving classic gentian-based drink that's perfect for a French-inspired cocktail hour or *apéro* at home.

1½ oz. Suze

Tonic water, to top

1. Pour the Suze into a highball or rocks glass, add ice, top with the tonic water, and stir slightly.
2. If desired, garnish with a strip of lemon zest.

MARLUSSE ET LAPIN

14 Rue Germain Pilon, 75018 Paris

It's fitting that the little entryway of this funky Pigalle bar is all red because it's literally the bullseye that a fun-seeking crowd of locals in their late teens and early twenties aims straight for. These party people are mainly drawn by the cheap pints, which are even cheaper during happy hour, but the decor has a certain appeal as well. While the entry room is relatively nondescript, the back room is decked out like your grandmother's one-room apartment complete with a clawfoot tub and an old, heavy bed frame reconfigured as seating. Faded wallpaper, a wardrobe, and sewing machine complete the dusty picture.

At Marlusse et Lapin, the staff is mostly as young and fun-loving as the clientele, all of whom are not yet worn down by time or jaded with life. There is lots of laughter. And all of that youthful joie de vivre gets a little rowdy and a little loud. Especially when the cheap vodka and juice cocktails start flowing, Belgian beers are on the go, and the specialty shots are being set afire.

To experience this space but sidestep some of the more disorderly elements, grab a rickety stool at the wooden bar in the front room. Here, the crowd is a little quieter and a few older habitues shoot the breeze with the bartenders.

Amidst all this carefree chaos, you may be pleasantly surprised to discover the beautiful belle époque reproduction absinthe fountain on the bar. And, Marlusse et Lapin stocks a few quality bottles to put it to use, making this a good place in which to dance with the green fairy. Not all know not to light the sugar cube on fire, however. In fact, this is the kind of place that adheres to a "the more fire, the better" kind of tenet. So, if you don't want them to put on the show with this customary but historically inaccurate gimmick that can leave your drink tasting like burnt sugar, keep an eye on their prep.

SUNSET

100 Rue Ordener, 75018 Paris

Visitors to Montmartre tend to concentrate on the touristy side of this popular destination, from the Sacré-Coeur down to the busy Boulevard Clichy. But the back side of the Butte Montmartre is where the real local life lives. This stretch is less expensive, more residential, and offers better opportunities to hang with Parisians doing their regular thing at places like Sunset.

Built in what was formerly a beer hall, there is plenty of space for separate restaurant and bar areas. And it's Paris, so of course there is a terrace too. When the neighbors aren't in for meals, they're in for drinks. Afternoon is popular for their *goûter*, which means afternoon snack, and is a weekday post-school ritual for all French children. But anyone can enjoy a *goûter*, like the adults who drop in here around 4 p.m. for this specially priced combo of a hot drink and a dessert. A little later, regulars order the *planche* special, a charcuterie plate plus the "wine of the moment" at a nice price. The beer is artisanal, the wine is natural, and the cocktails are inventive, sometimes employing vegetal elements like cucumber or bell pepper.

The decor is modern and fresh with an industrial feel that is softened by the colorful wall paint job done by artist Matthieu Cossé, also a resident of the 18th. Open space, big windows, clean lines, and lots of table and counter space give off a slight whiff of café-diner.

EN VRAC

2 Rue de l'Olive, 75018 Paris

The name En Vrac means "in bulk" and, as that suggests, the team puts in the time and effort to source high-quality wine in large formats. They then pass that savings onto customers who come to taste test at the bar and take consignment bottles or boxes of their favorites home.

Tucked away on a lesser traveled corner of Montmartre, the space is laid-back and casual with a rustic feel and youthful energy. Silver tanks of bulk wine line one wall and a bottle tree is generally in service to drain and dry the washed empties waiting to be refilled and sent back into rotation. Savvy locals bring their own containers to be filled.

The location and the ethos of the establishment draw a crowd of mainly thirty- to fortysomething Parisians who keep on top of what is happening in the food and drinks world and also appreciate the easy-going vibe

The food is simple, such as rustic plates of cheese and charcuterie or the fresh Normandy oysters available on the weekends when in season. The wine leans toward the natural end of the spectrum and locals come to learn more about it at dedicated wine-blending work-shops. The bar also goes beyond wine with local ciders, growlers of beer, Italian Prosecco, and a small selection of spirits in bulk.

So do yourself a favor and drink better for less in Paris. Either settle in at the bar or make like a local and grab a to-go bottle or box and take it to your nearest park for a picnic.

SUPERCOIN

17 Rue Boinod, 75018 Paris

Founded by a trio of early adopters of the artisanal brewing trend, Supercoin helped convince a skeptical French public used to industrial lagers that beer could be made better. They opened their simple, and slightly divey, location in 2012, offering eight or so artisanal French microbrews on tap alongside an international selection of whisky.

Thanks to their quality domestic draughts and a burgeoning craft beer scene that they helped nurture, their client base grew and they were eventually able to move to their bigger, nicer space. Their cute forest green bar with its busy terrace is still located a little off the beaten path on a tight corner at the back side of Montmartre with a rotating list of beers on tap as well as plenty of bottled options. They also offer fun food like egg, sausage, or veggie sandwiches. And all of this at very reasonable prices.

The above should be enough to keep the masses happy, but Supercoin goes beyond. The team has always been crafty at capitalizing on and further fostering the beer-loving population. They get involved at the city's annual beer festival and collaborate with others on special releases. But it goes beyond the beer. Supercoin has an agenda of activities that keeps the customers engaged and entertained on a regular basis, including karaoke, bar quizzes, DJ sets, and workshops. The engagement also goes beyond the four walls with social media intended not just to keep followers informed but to relate to them as members of a community. They're not just folks trying to sell you a fancy beer. They are also your friends. And that's the kind of local that is drawn to this down-to-earth bar.

LUSH

16 Rue des Dames, 75017 Paris

O f all the bars in this book, Lush is the one I've spent the most time in, but currently know the least about. Lush was the first bar I went to after moving to Paris. Situated just steps from my front door, it became a near daily stop. I'd poke my head in on my way home from work or come for company in the evening because there was always someone I knew sitting at, or standing behind, the bar.

The founders, Ken O'Reilly and Jim Marshall, put a lot of heart, soul, and time into the bar, often working behind it themselves, as new owners are wont to do. And in doing so they built a community of regulars who came to watch the match, celebrate a birthday, or just decompress from the day all in the good company of friends.

These days, most of my Lush friends have families, busy jobs, or have moved to other parts of the city, country, and world. We still meet regularly, but we have less time for endless evenings in the bar. Our circumstances have changed, but so has the bar. And that's what makes it a real, living venue that, rather than staying static, morphs with the lives of those who animate it. Now a new crop of fresh-faced friends is making their own lifelong memories here.

Lush attracts a healthy mash-up of French and international expats who live nearby. The laughter coming from the usually open door, and the unusual relief sculpture wood panels on the front also pull in a smattering of interesting tourists from the fun, funky, affordable hotel next door. Once I even found myself sitting next to iconic 1980s' actress Mary Stewart Masterson during an impromptu singalong at the bar.

It's also a good gateway to the 17th arrondissement, the out of the way sidewalks of which are packed with Parisians. Hip BBQ joints, bars, and boutiques are mushrooming on its streets, but thanks to its proximity to the city's outskirts this remains very native drinking territory. The nearby beautiful Batignolles park and square are surrounded by neighborhood bars so numerous they are hardly worth naming individually. But Lush is a good starting point.

19th & 20th Arrondissements
Buttes Chaumont / Belleville / Père Lachaise

Apart from the popular Père Lachaise, these out of the way areas go largely unexplored by tourists who miss out on this peek behind the curtain at real Parisian life. The bars here reflect the spunk and individuality of the neighborhood residents who frequent them.

17th

16th

7

15th

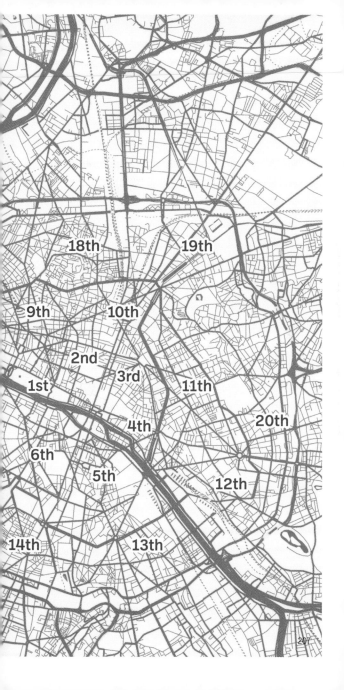

COMBAT

63 Rue de Belleville, 75019 Paris

It takes guts and talent to successfully open a cocktail bar in the less polished corners of Paris. Fortunately Combat owner, Margot Lecarpentier, has enough of both to have set up shop in the diverse, at times disorderly, working-class Belleville neighborhood.

Belleville is home to many of the city's immigrants, migrants, artistic types, and bourgeois bohemians snapping up cheap real estate where life unfolds in a less picturesque, more realistically gritty way, which can sometimes be unnerving to the uninitiated. It's a different perspective on Paris, but just as real an aspect of the city as the postcard-perfect parts. Combat takes its name from the ancient moniker of the neighborhood in which it resides, as well as reflecting the feminist struggle for equality.

This cheerfully minimalist bar is a breath of fresh air that stands out not just within its chaotic location, but amongst its many peers all over Paris. It's open and airy and it's hard not to smile when staring at the canary yellow—tiled back wall from across the clean metal bar. It's a testament to a less-is-more approach. There is no need for extra fuss and muss with sound underlying foundations of quality and principle.

Lecarpentier previously worked at some of the city's best bars, is author of *La bible des alcools*, and was awarded Most Influential Bartender at the 2019 Paris Cocktails Spirits salon. She's clearly got some serious cocktail cred. So does the full bar team that regularly puts together a solid menu that has all the hallmarks of high-quality craft cocktails, like house-made ingredients, well-selected spirits, and a balance both in the glass and across the full spectrum of drinks.

It's also the kind of business that combines its owner's personal principles with strong ecologically sensitive

and sustainable practices and all-inclusive policies. The result is a bar with soul and character that is socially and environmentally clued in, and still turning out damn good drinks.

All of the above explain why the tiny sidewalk terrace and the open indoor space are consistently packed with both locals and the occasional in-the-know visiting cocktail enthusiast.

QUATRESSE

The Quatresse exemplifies the less-is-more approach at Combat, with a few, easy to source ingredients that come together for a showstopper of a cocktail.

1⅔ oz. Suze

⅔ oz. fresh lemon juice

2 tsp. simple syrup

8 dashes Laphroaig Whisky

2 sage leaves

1. Combine all of the ingredients in a cocktail shaker with ice, shake well for 10 to 15 seconds, and double strain into a large rocks glass.
2. Garnish with another sage leaf.

ROSA BONHEUR BUTTES CHAUMONT

2 Av. de la Cascade, 75019 Paris

*G*uinguettes are open-air dance halls and drinking establishments that were very popular in France in the nineteenth century. Usually on the water, they sprung up in summer months on the outskirts of cities where lower taxes meant cheaper drinking. These rowdy, festive, working-class venues eventually fell out of fashion and the few that remained were nostalgic throwbacks where older couples waltzed to dated music. But Rosa Bonheur revitalized this French tradition with a contemporary take on the old *guinguette*.

While it may be a bit out of the way, it's worth heading to Rosa Bonheur Butte Chaumont for the setting alone. Located in one of Paris's biggest parks, complete with caves, hills, waterfalls, and plenty of trees, it really recalls a sense of the past when *guinguettes* were located on the fringes of cities.

Rosa Bonheur serves inexpensive tapas-style snacks and easy drinks to accompany the themed evenings, concerts, tea dances, music, and more. The crowd may be updated and the music a little more modern, but the same sense of revelry and pleasure found in the *guinguettes* of another era prevails. One of the founders previously owned a popular lesbian bar in Paris, and

Rosa Bonheur cultivates an all-inclusive ethos that has given this spot a strong reputation within the LGBTQ+ community as well.

And although this delightful drinking and dance hall is far from the center of town, people still come in droves. It's a destination on its own and also draws in those looking for a post-picnic drink or some sustenance before walking the extensive grounds around it. Young and carefree locals who come here are willing to wait in long lines to gain access. Being a victim of its own success does, however, have an upside. They've subsequently opened three other *guinguettes* around Paris, including one on a Seine riverboat.

LE PAVILLON DES CANAUX

39 Quai de la Loire, 75019 Paris

Le Pavillon des Canaux has been a part of the Canal de l'Ourcq landscape for over a century, originally serving as home to the canal's onsite locks inspector. Decades later, after falling into disuse and disrepair, this charming two-story building got a new lease on life with an imaginative, colorful renovation.

The overhaul of this building began with idealistic inspirations. The intention was to create an all-inclusive supportive space with lofty ambitions, like fostering equality, diversity, respect for the environment, and appreciation for sustainable practices. The goal was a space between work and home, a comfy limbo that could spark creativity and reinforce community.

The design agency initially left the interior like a house. The different rooms are decorated with cute-as-a-button style. Bright colors reign and whimsical touches abound in this life-sized dollhouse. Guests can settle into one of the comfy bedrooms with friends over drinks or open their laptop at the kitchen table for a coffee and catch up on work. The clawfoot tub is a highly sought-after spot to recline with a beer and a book.

To further engage the community, the Pavillon des Canaux hosts a series of events such as workshops, art exhibits, and other social activities. In line with their eco-friendly ethos they feature beers, ciders, wines, and coffee from France. Chai tea and playful cocktails round out the drinks menu. At lunch they serve a soup and salad type of menu and cold snacks in the evening.

It's a place where idealistic youth debate and discuss how to make the world a better place over bottles of artisanal beer. It's also a place where the chill crowd comes to contemplate the canal over a glass of rosé on the covered terrace. In line with their fundamental goals, it's more than just a spot for a drink, but a place where everyone feels welcome as long as they keep an open mind and heart.

More Fun Spots Off the Beaten Path

LA COMMUNE
80 Bd de Belleville, 75020 Paris

LES TRIPLETTES
102 Bd de Belleville, 75020 Paris

LA BELLEVILLOISE
19-21 Rue Boyer, 75020 Paris

PANAME
41 bis Quai de la Loire, 75019 Paris

Acknowledgments

Writing this took a lot of work, which was made much easier by many other people.

Thanks to my friends and contacts who offered suggestions for their favorite local spots for the book and/or have regularly gotten on the ground for drinks research with me: Zeva Bellel, Jane Bertch, Gail Boisclair, Luke Bryan, Violaine Chapelle, Chris Ewing, Sébastien Foulard, Jane Grey, Lily Heise, Frederick Hume, David Lebovitz, Susan Herrmann Loomis, Laurence Marot, Emily Monaco, Matt Mulot, Thibaut Neuman, Anna Newsome, Carole Nicolas, Declan O'Meara, Anthony Poncier, Kate Ross, Scott Schuder, Heather Stimmler, Tanisha Townsend, Melanie Vaz, Lisa White, and Wendy Willis Miller.

Extra thanks to my friends who did the above and also went beyond to review my entries that fall into their areas of expertise or interest: Allison Zinder (for Belleville and *guinguettes*), Emily Dilling (for craft beer bars), and Cliodhna Fullam, Nicola Flanagan, and Jennifer Greco (for neighborhood descriptions).

Cheers to all the people name-checked in the book and also those who aren't but work in or own the drinking establishments listed in these pages.

Warm thanks to Buzz Poole and the team at HarperCollins for giving me the opportunity to write the guide.

My biggest thanks to my favorite local, Thibault Devillers, who was the most patient and biggest source of support through the process. (*Je t'aime.*)

About the Author

Cocktail expert Forest Collins founded 52martinis.com in 2007 to chronicle her search for the best cocktail bars in Paris and cover other small-batch spirits news from France. She is the creator of the iOS app Paris Cocktails and host of the radio show and podcast *Paris Cocktails Talk*. She has written for *Drinks International*, Serious Eats, World's Best Bars, and other websites and publications. Collins is the academy chair for France for the World's 50 Best Bars and president of the France chapter of the Les Dames d'Escoffier. And she's also a pretty fun drinking partner.

About Cider Mill Press
Book Publishers

Good ideas ripen with time. From seed to harvest, Cider Mill Press strives to bring fine reading, information, and entertainment together between the covers of its creatively crafted books. Our Cider Mill bears fruit twice a year, publishing a new crop of titles each spring and fall.

"Where good books are ready for press"
501 Nelson Place
Nashville, Tennessee 37214

cidermillpress.com